A taste of
Cumbria
The Lake District

First published 2008
by ncjMedia Ltd
Groat Market,
Newcastle upon Tyne, NE1 1ED
ISBN 9780955236037

Editors: Kathryn Armstrong, Katharine Capocci
Design Editor: Ian Guy
Design team: Sarah Mullaney, Kevin Waddell
Sales manager: Duncan Peters

Tableware: Crosby's, www.crosbys.co.uk

Printed by Journal Print Media Ltd of Dunlop Way, Scunthorpe, DN16 3RN

North East
exclusive

A taste of
Cumbria
The Lake District

Photography by Nicky Rogerson and Kevin Gibson

CONTENTS

FOREWORD

As a Cumbrian it gives me great pleasure to write this introduction. We have great food in Cumbria and I am proud and excited to celebrate it.

Firstly, it makes sense to thank our food producers – the farmers and growers, without whom we would have no produce to eat and cook. We should be proud of our farmers. They have fought back from foot-and-mouth, changed with the times, and thanks to outlets like farmers' markets, great Cumbrian butchers, and supermarkets like Booths, we have world-class produce to eat and to cook.

Everything we could wish for is made by local artisan producers in Cumbria. Think pickles, ice-cream, great smokehouses and game, jams and cheese, to name but a few. Quite simply, no region does this better.

Publications like this serve to inspire you to have a go and try what is out there. I love the way, in Cumbria, we have so much choice – even our Michelin-starred restaurants are of such different character and venues, that there is something for everybody.

This is a region with great culinary tradition, going back to the days of Whitehaven being a spice port, giving us our gingerbread and wonderful, unique spicy Cumberland sausage. Undoubtedly we continue to have great home cooking, but now we live in one of the most exciting regions in the country in which to eat out.

We live in a beautiful place and thankfully great chefs from all over the world are drawn to live and work here because of the passion and excitement for our food. Local chefs have great seasonal local produce to use – after all why buy from away when we have the best at home? The face of the licensing industry has also had to change and many of our pubs and inns have risen to the challenge, and with creative chefs are giving us great local food without destroying our lovely Cumbrian pubs.

So go on, take this book, dive in and have a great adventure. It is all here on our doorstep.

Dave Myers

TV's Hairy Biker, born in Barrow-in-Furness, Cumbria

BROADOAKS
COUNTRY HOUSE

BROAD OAKS

COUNTRY HOUSE

MORNING COFFEE
LUNCHES
LICENSED

BROADOAKS COUNTRY HOUSE

Broadoaks has been a privately-run country house hotel for the last 16 years. It was originally built in 1835 for a military gentleman to reside in during his summer breaks. It was sold in the early 1890s to a doctor with a great passion for music who added on the beautiful Arts and Craft styled music room, complete with ornate plaster work by William Morris in 1905. Broadoaks was taken over in 2007 by Tracey Robinson and Paula Glacken. With a passion for design and five-star boutique hotels the pair have transformed the house in keeping with the original features and with period design direction from the KLC school of design in London.

The Oaks Restaurant: Head chef Taran Baxter from Ficksburg, South Africa and sous chef Ryon Tyson from Ocho Rios, Jamaica have worked in fine dining kitchens across the world. These influences and their love of traditional Cumbrian food have led to a fantastic selection of modern dishes with nuances of the area's traditional cuisine.

Our menu changes daily with a range of Taran's signature dishes available from Friday to Sunday. We cater for all requirements; bespoke menus are created upon request for restaurant and wedding parties and we have specific menus for coeliac and lactose-intolerant customers. Broadoaks delivers a fine but unfussy dining experience with a vast wine list from quality houses throughout Europe and the New World. A fantastic selection of local cheeses, port and dessert wines offers a choice and variety that is often missed.

Tracey Robinson and Paula Glacken, proprietors

BROADOAKS
COUNTRY HOUSE

Grilled Kyle of Lochalsh langoustines dressed with Morecambe Bay potted shrimps and garlic parsley butter

Serves 1

INGREDIENTS

2 whole langoustines

1 clove garlic, finely chopped

1 tsp finely chopped parsley

1 tsp shrimps

knob melted butter

dash of olive oil

METHOD

Drop langoustines in boiling water for two minutes.
Then plunge into cold water to cool.
Cut the langoustines down the middle from head to tail. Place langoustines on a baking tray. In a small pan heat together the butter, oil, shrimps and garlic.
Drizzle some sauce over the langoustines and place under the grill for a few minutes.
Arrange on a warm plate and garnish with chopped parsley and lemon.

BROADOAKS

*Bridge Lane, Troutbeck, Windermere, Cumbria, LA23 1LA
Tel: 015394 45566, www.broadoakscountryhouse.co.uk*

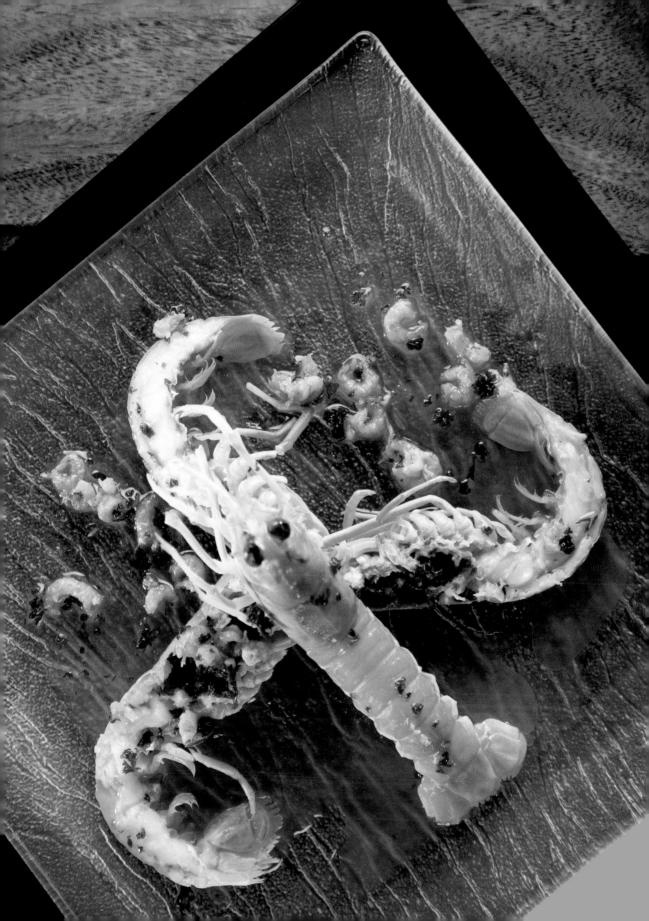

BROADOAKS
COUNTRY HOUSE

Aberdeen Angus fillet tower

Serves 4

FILLET:
4 x 170g//6oz Aberdeen Angus fillet
steak

SAUCE:
2 medium shallots
6 medium mushrooms
$^1/_2$ pint demi glaze
1 tsp French mustard
good dash of cognac
dash of double cream

ROSTI:
4 large potatoes
handful grated cheddar cheese
sprinkle of chopped parsley
salt and pepper
1 tsp oil
knob of butter

MUSHROOM PATE:
12 medium mushrooms
slosh of Shiraz
knob of butter
salt and pepper

For the sauce, dice the shallots, sauté in a pan with butter, then add the mushrooms to the shallots and sauté until soft. Next add the cognac and flambé then add the demi glaze and French mustard and bring to the boil. Stir in the cream and season to taste.

For the mushroom pate, finely dice the mushrooms and sauté with butter. Add the Shiraz and season. Bring to the boil; leave to simmer until the mixture has reduced to a slightly coarse pate consistency.

For rosti, add potato to boiling water. Boil for five minutes. Refresh potato in cold water and leave to cool. Grate the cold potato into a bowl and add the grated cheese and parsley. Season to taste. In a frying pan heat four teaspoons of oil and add the potato mixture. Fry potato mixture on both sides until golden brown. Cut out into two-inch rounds.

Fillet, cut the 6oz fillets into three equal portions. Season each medallion. Heat a little oil in a pan. Sear the medallions on both sides.

Assembly, place rosti on a plate then top with fillet medallion, spoon the mushroom pate in between each medallion. Drizzle with the sauce and serve with seasonal vegetables.

BROADOAKS

*Bridge Lane, Troutbeck, Windermere, Cumbria, LA23 1LA
Tel: 015394 45566, www.broadoakscountryhouse.co.uk*

BROADOAKS
COUNTRY HOUSE

Raspberry and Drambuie-infused Pavlova

Serves 4

INGREDIENTS

MERINGUE:

3 egg whites

170g/6oz caster sugar

2 tsp cornflour

1 tsp malt vinegar

¹/₂ tsp vanilla essence

RASPBERRIES:

1 x 500g bag of frozen raspberries

dash of Drambuie

4oz caster sugar

METHOD

Add the raspberries, Drambuie and caster sugar together in a bowl and leave to infuse. Pre-heat the oven to 130C. Whisk the egg whites until stiff, gradually adding the sugar. Continue whisking until thick and glossy. Whisk in the cornflour, vinegar and vanilla essence. Spoon the meringue into a piping bag and pipe eight three-inch rounds onto a lined baking tray. Bake for approximately 40 minutes until firm.

Assembly, place one meringue onto a decorated plate, pipe a little cream into the centre then top with another round. Spoon a generous amount of raspberries onto the meringue and spoon a little raspberry juice over the top. Decorate with spun sugar.

BROADOAKS

Bridge Lane, Troutbeck, Windermere, Cumbria, LA23 1LA
Tel: 015394 45566, www.broadoakscountryhouse.co.uk

THE COTTAGE
IN THE WOOD

THE COTTAGE IN THE WOOD

The Cottage in the Wood is a 17th Century former coaching inn located on magic hill in the heart of Whinlatter, England's only mountain forest and amidst the fells of the North West Lakes. The Cottage provides a beautiful and tranquil location. The restaurant has been refurbished and extended during 2008 and the terrace and conservatory provide stunning views of the forest valley and the mighty Skiddaw mountain range.

Like many restaurants in the region, we make full use of a vast array of local ingredients. Without doubt, no better lamb or mutton can be found than that reared on the Lakeland fells. Fresh, top quality fish and shellfish is available from Maryport, just thirty minutes' drive away and we make the most of the wild foods we harvest from the forest.

Our philosophy towards food is to secure the best possible local and seasonal produce and to cook it simply and creatively. Ethical farming is important to us and we aim to ensure all our practices are friendly to the environment.

Kath and Liam Berney

THE COTTAGE IN THE WOOD

Smoked haddock and saffron tart
with rocket and Parmesan salad

Serves 8

INGREDIENTS

500g good quality smoked haddock (undyed), skinned and cut into 1cm dice

good pinch saffron

100ml milk

300ml double cream

6 free-range egg yolks

salt and ground black pepper

RICH SHORTCRUST PASTRY:

500g soft flour

250g unsalted butter

tsp salt (omit if using salted butter)

2 egg yolks

200ml ice-cold water

TO GARNISH:

150g rocket leaves

50g Parmesan shavings

METHOD

Preparation, make the pastry well in advance. Crumb the flour with 1cm cubes of butter. This works well in a food processor, but make sure the butter is very cold. Add the eggs and water (and salt if using) and quickly combine. Roll into a cylinder on a floured surface, divide into four equal pieces (approx 230g-250g), wrap in film and leave to rest in a fridge for at least 30 minutes. Take one piece of pastry and roll out as thinly as possible (2-3mm) on a lightly floured surface. Lift and turn frequently to avoid the pastry sticking to the surface. Line one 20cm flan ring with the pastry or eight 8cm individual non-stick tartlet tins. (If you use tartlet tins, be prepared to roll out the trimmings remaining from your pastry, or break into another of the stored pieces). The remaining pastry pieces can now be frozen for future use. Add the cream, milk and saffron to a pan and heat gently to simmering point. In the meantime, put the yolks into a mixing bowl and whisk together. Pour on the hot saffron cream mixture whilst gently whisking. Season and leave to stand for ten minutes.

Cooking, sprinkle the diced haddock evenly onto the prepared flan ring or tartlets. Pour on the saffron cream and bake in a pre-heated oven (180C or gas mark 4). Remove from the oven when lightly baked. Leave to stand until cool enough to handle, then carefully remove onto a cooling wire.

Serving, the tart can be refrigerated for up to 24 hours prior to serving. When required, place on a lightly greased tray and bake in hot oven (220C or gas mark 6) for ten minutes or so, until the pastry crisps. Allow to cool a little before serving. Portion onto plates and garnish with rocket and parmesan.

THE COTTAGE IN THE WOOD

Magic Hill, Braithwaite, Nr Keswick, Cumbria, CA12 5TW
Tel: 017687 78409, www.thecottageinthewood.co.uk

THE COTTAGE IN THE WOOD

Loin of fell-bred lamb roasted with lemon & thyme with Pinot Noir gravy, wild garlic and St George's mushrooms

Serves 4

INGREDIENTS

2 short loins of lamb, around 500g each	50g butter
200g mirepoix, roughly diced (¹/₂ cm)	1 tspn flour
carrot, onion and celery	250ml good red Burgundy or New
thyme stalks	Zealand Pinot Noir
splash of oil	250ml chicken stock
grated zest of lemon	200g St George's mushrooms or similar
sprig of thyme, picked and chopped	100g wild garlic leaves (use baby
100g white breadcrumbs	spinach or pak choi as an alternative)

METHOD

Preparation, make sure the butcher has included the bones from lamb loins. You can ask him or her to chop them. Prepare lamb loins by removing fat coating. Trim off connective tissue (silvery skin). Cover and place in fridge. Make lemon and thyme coating. Add 50g of butter to a frying pan and heat until frothy. Add breadcrumbs and stir over gentle heat until golden brown. Add lemon zest and thyme whilst still warm. Measure out 250ml of the good red wine. Cut mushrooms in half, or quarters. Wash and dry wild garlic leaves. **Cooking,** season lamb loins. Heat frying pan and add oil. When oil begins to smoke, add loins of lamb and leave for 30-40 seconds to allow meat to seal and brown. Turn over, and apply to other side. Turn off heat and remove loins from pan. Wipe out pan and again heat pan and more oil. Add chopped lamb bones and other trimmings, and allow to brown. Add mirepoix (roughly diced carrot, onion & celery) and this should also colour a little without burning. Finally, sprinkle on flour. Position browned bones in middle of pan to allow lamb joints to sit on them. Roll the lamb joints in crumb, lemon and thyme mixture and sit on the bones. Place in preheated oven (180C/gas mark 4) for six to eight minutes. Turn over and return to oven for a further six to eight minutes, or until meat is cooked 'pink.' Remove from oven and allow lamb joints to rest for five minutes. Gradually add red wine to roasting pan, stirring and bringing to boil each time. Repeat this process with chicken stock, until you have a smooth, slightly thickened gravy. Strain through a fine sieve into a clean pan and cover until required. **Service,** place a little butter in a frying pan and heat until frothy, add the mushrooms. When mushrooms partially cooked, add wild garlic leaves and allow these to wilt over a gentle heat. The steam from the wild garlic will finish cooking mushrooms. Divide between four plates. Slice each lamb joint into six pieces and dress each plate with a portion of three slices. Warm through and spoon red wine gravy around plate.

THE COTTAGE IN THE WOOD

Magic Hill, Braithwaite, Nr Keswick, Cumbria, CA12 5TW
Tel: 017687 78409, www.thecottageinthewood.co.uk

THE COTTAGE IN THE WOOD

Lemon yoghurt cream with raspberries

Serves 6

250g rich shortcrust pastry or
8 discs of sponge

3 lemons

50g caster sugar

3 leaves gelatine (soaked in cold water)
(or 1 level tbsp of powdered)

200ml Greek yoghurt

150ml whipping cream

250g British raspberries

**RASPBERRY &
RED WINE SAUCE:**

500g frozen raspberries

200g caster sugar

250ml red wine

1 lemon, juiced

EQUIPMENT:

6 x 70mm mousse rings

METHOD

Preparation, firstly, make the raspberry and red wine sauce. This can be made a day or so in advance and will produce a sufficient quantity to be saved and used again. Simply combine the ingredients and simmer for a few moments. Liquidise and pass through a fine sieve to remove the seeds. Allow to cool and store in a fridge. Roll out the pastry to a thickness of 5mm and cut out six discs using a mousse ring, bake in a hot oven (220C) on parchment or similar for ten minutes or until golden brown. Alternatively, you may wish to use discs of sponge. Place the pastry or sponge discs inside the mousse rings and cover with raspberries. On a tray, place these in the fridge in readiness for the yoghurt cream. To make the yoghurt creams, firstly remove the zest with a fine grater and squeeze the juice from the lemons. In a small pan, reduce the juice by half. Dissolve the gelatine into the warm juice and strain through a sieve into a bowl. Thoroughly mix in the yoghurt with a whisk and then place this lemon yoghurt mixture into the fridge in order to chill and set lightly. With a spatula, stir from the sides of the bowl frequently. In the meantime, whip the cream lightly to a stage whereby it just peaks. When the lemon yoghurt mixture begins to set, lightly fold in the whipped cream. Pour the mixture into the mousse rings and over the raspberries, return to the 'fridge for at least four hours in order to set.

Serving, remove the yoghurt creams from the fridge and quickly warm the mousse rings, run the tip of a warm knife around the rim of the moulds to release the rings. Carefully lift the ring to release the yoghurt creams. Spread a little of the raspberry and red wine sauce on six plates and carefully place a yoghurt cream on each. Dress with the remainder of the raspberries.

THE COTTAGE IN THE WOOD

Magic Hill, Braithwaite, Nr Keswick, Cumbria, CA12 5TW
Tel: 017687 78409, www.thecottageinthewood.co.uk

DALE LODGE HOTEL

DALE LODGE HOTEL

Dale Lodge Hotel and Tweedies Bar was taken over by the Roberts family in May 2004. Much work has been undertaken since then to build a reputation of quality service and excellent food. The hotel itself has undergone a dramatic change from an old-fashioned, traditional place to something contemporary, clean and spacious.

The food which is passionately created by head chef James Goodall is of a classic style with a continental twist. James trained in London from the age of 16 before working in France, Spain and Australia where he gained some excellent experience and masses of inspiration which comes through in his work today. He returned to his home in the Lake District in 2002 and before opening Dale Lodge, was head chef at The Log House Restaurant in Ambleside. The Lake District fells, being a great natural resource for rearing livestock, produces some of the best meat around. Our seasonally changing menus reflect this, with some fabulous game dishes in the winter months and the most succulent spring-time lamb and local char.

In Tweedies Bar our full menu is available in more informal surroundings. With a large range of award-winning real ales, extensive wine list and possibly the largest beer garden in the Lake District, Tweedies Bar is a wonderful place for a light lunch, family gathering or special occasion The more intimate setting of The Lodge Restaurant is set within the main hotel. The sumptuous surroundings, flickering candlelight and personal service make for a perfect and memorable evening.

Brian and Gillian Roberts, proprietors

DALE LODGE HOTEL

Shredded duck, wild mushroom and white truffle oil terrine wrapped in leeks and served with a pear and saffron chutney

Serves 8

INGREDIENTS

8 large duck legs

4 cloves garlic

2 sprigs thyme

1kg duck fat

25g butter

8 leeks

100g mixed wild mushrooms

100g butter

2 cloves garlic

10ml white truffle oil

50g chopped chives,

50g chopped parsley

FOR SAFFRON CHUTNEY:

6 pears

$\frac{1}{2}$g saffron

100g sugar

5g fennel seeds

500g golden raisins

20ml cider vinegar

METHOD

To confit the duck legs, place roasting tray on stove and add the duck fat, duck legs, garlic, thyme and 25g butter, cover with tin foil and cook in a pre-heated oven at 150C for two-and-a-half hours. Once cooked remove the duck legs from the tray and leave to cool for 15 minutes before removing the skin. Shred the duck meat away from the bone using a couple of forks. Allow to cool then add the chopped chives, seasoning and parsley.

To make the terrine, chill the terrine mould and line with cling film. Remove the white from the leek, slice longways and remove the large outer leaves. Blanch in boiling water for around 15 seconds, remove from the water and allow to cool before lining the terrine dish with them, leaving the strands over-hanging the edge of the dish to be folded over the bottom of the terrine when full. Prepare and wash the mushrooms before placing them in a hot pan with the butter and white truffle oil, cook until soft then allow to cool. Next, layer up the terrine dish first with shredded duck, then the mushrooms until the terrine is full. The bottom layer should also be duck. Cover with the leeks and cling film and press overnight before serving.

For the chutney, peel the pears, core and chop into even half centimetre cubes. Heat the cider vinegar, fennel seeds and sugar in a pan, add the saffron, pears and raisins. Cover with a lid and let this cook out on a gentle heat for about an hour until it binds together. Allow to cool before serving.

DALE LODGE HOTEL

Grasmere, Cumbria, LA22 9SW
Tel: 015394 35300, www.dalelodgehotel.co.uk

DALE LODGE HOTEL

Pan-fried halibut with creamed leeks, saffron turned new potatoes, baby fennel and king scallops in a fish velouté

Serves 4

INGREDIENTS

4 6oz/170g portions of halibut	
2 leeks	
8 baby fennel	
$^1/_2$ g saffron	
16 medium-sized new potatoes	
25g butter	
1 clove garlic	

FOR VELOUTÉ:

150ml double cream

200ml fish stock

100ml Martini Bianco

METHOD

Take the 16 new potatoes and peel them from end to end until they are all the same size. Put the saffron in a pan of boiling water, add the potatoes and cook for 20 minutes until soft.

Place a saucepan on a low heat. Take the shallots, finely slice them and place them in the hot pan with a little olive oil and one clove of garlic. Add the Martini and allow this to reduce by half, then add the fish stock and reduce this by half again. Finally add the cream and a little salt and pepper to taste.

Cut the leeks in half lengthways and rinse under cold water. Cut them into equal sized pieces about 1cm thick and blanch in boiling water for about four minutes. Put 25ml cream and 25g butter in a pan on a low heat, add the part-cooked leeks and cook until they bind together. Take the fennel and trim off any damaged outer leaves, blanch this in boiling water for about six minutes and finish by frying in a little butter for a further couple of minutes.

Heat a large non-stick frying pan and add a little olive oil. Season your fish and place in the pan. Cook for three minutes then add 25g unsalted butter, turn it over and cook for another three minutes.

Take a frying pan with a little olive oil in and put it on a high heat. Add the scallops and cook for one minute on each side. Finish off by melting in a knob of butter.

DALE LODGE HOTEL

Grasmere, Cumbria, LA22 9SW
Tel: 015394 35300, www.dalelodgehotel.co.uk

DALE LODGE HOTEL

Roast rack of Cumbrian Herdwick lamb with butternut squash puree, Dauphinois potatoes, marinated artichokes and a Madeira and white truffle jus

Serves 6

INGREDIENTS

2 whole Herdwick lamb racks
- French trimmed
2 sprigs rosemary
2 cloves garlic
12 baby artichoke hearts

FOR DAUPHINOIS:

6 large King Edward potatoes
200ml cream
2 cloves garlic
2 sprigs thyme
50g butter
pinch sea salt
pinch cracked black pepper

FOR SAUCE:

25ml Madeira
150ml good quality beef stock
2 chopped shallots
1 sprig rosemary

FOR PUREE:

1 large butternut squash
1 clove garlic
10ml cream
salt and pepper
olive oil

METHOD

Butternut puree, cut the butternut squash in half and remove the seeds. Place in a roasting tray and cover lightly in olive oil, 25g butter, salt and pepper, then put it in a pre-heated oven at 200C for 20 minutes until soft. Remove from the oven, peel off the skin and place in a blender with one clove of garlic and 10ml cream. Once pureed pass through a sieve, add 20g melted butter. **For potatoes,** place 200ml cream, chopped garlic and thyme on the stove and bring to boil. Remove from heat and allow flavours to infuse. Peel the potatoes and thinly slice them with either a mandolin or very sharp knife. Layer the potatoes in a roasting tray, putting a little of the cream between each layer. Slice 25g butter on top and put in the oven at 180C for 40-60 minutes until soft. Remove from oven, allow it to cool. Press for half an hour before cutting to shape. **For sauce,** put the chopped shallots into a hot pan, add the Madeira and simmer. Add beef stock and simmer until reduced by half, add the chopped rosemary. **For lamb,** cut racks into three and remove half of the fat. Score the flesh and leave to rest. Heat a pan and place seasoned racks and rosemary in pan, seal meat on all sides and then place in oven at 200C for about 20 minutes for medium rare. Put the artichoke hearts in a roasting tray and drizzle with olive oil, cook these for 20 minutes at 200C. Remove from oven, rest for a few minutes in a warm place, slice racks in half and serve.

DALE LODGE HOTEL

Grasmere, Cumbria, LA22 9SW
Tel: 015394 35300, www.dalelodgehotel.co.uk

THE GLASS HOUSE
RESTAURANT

THE GLASS HOUSE RESTAURANT

The Glass House Restaurant, Ambleside lies at the centre of this most beautiful corner of England and at its culinary heart. The restaurant occupies a cleverly restored Grade II listed building dating from the 15th Century that operated as a fulling mill. When the mill was refurbished in 1995, the working weir, millrace, wheel and various pieces of machinery were carefully retained and an impressive oak framework was introduced to provide a series of imaginative mezzanine floors.

As for the food, we use the freshest local produce from the Lakeland fells and farms, and fuse classic British dishes with European menus. Freshness, quality and simplicity are our signature qualities. Our ingredients are always the best.

Atmosphere may not be edible but it does play a huge part in your dining enjoyment at the Glass House. Our friendly team serve in a refreshingly casual but attentive way to produce a relaxed, enjoyable ambience.

Neil Farrell

THE GLASS HOUSE RESTAURANT

Poached salmon salad

Serves 4

INGREDIENTS

2 fillets of salmon, skinned	1 fennel head
1 courgette	20 cherry tomatoes
28 fine beans	French dressing
¹/₂ red onion	balsamic vinegar

METHOD

Method, add salmon fillets to pan of cold water, bring to boil, after two minutes remove from heat and sit for four minutes and remove and allow to cool. Cook fine beans in boiling, salted water for five minutes, allow to cool. Cut courgette in half (top to bottom) and peel into ribbons. Finely slice onion and fennel, cut cherry tomatoes in half. Mix vegetables with French dressing and season in bowl. Flake salmon through salad and arrange onto plates, garnish with balsamic vinegar.

THE GLASS HOUSE RESTAURANT

Rydal Road, Ambleside, Cumbria, LA22 9AN
Tel: 015394 32137, www.theglasshouserestaurant.co.uk

THE GLASS HOUSE RESTAURANT

Braised Herdwick lamb

Serves 4

INGREDIENTS

4 lamb shoulders (Herdwick if possible)

3 carrots

1 onion

3 sticks of celery

1 litre vegetable stock

1/2 bottle of red wine

250g plain flour

3 sprigs rosemary

3 sprigs thyme

2 cloves garlic

100g tomato puree

METHOD

Method, place flour onto baking tray and roast until brown. Seal lamb in pan until dark brown on all sides and remove. Roughly cut vegetables and add to same pan, colour then add tomato puree. Add red wine and reduce by half, stir in flour, add herbs, garlic and stock. Add to oven-proof roasting tin, add lamb and foil completely. Cook for two-and-a-half hours at 165C or until the bones pull out easily. Serve with honey roast parsnips and Dauphinois potato or vegetable and potato of your choice.

THE GLASS HOUSE RESTAURANT

Rydal Road, Ambleside, Cumbria, LA22 9AN
Tel: 015394 32137, www.theglasshouserestaurant.co.uk

THE GLASS HOUSE RESTAURANT

Chocolate Marquise

Serves 4

INGREDIENTS

SPONGE:

5 eggs

125g sugar

125g flour

MARQUISE MIX:

100g dark chocolate

65g butter

2 egg yolks

2 egg whites

40g sugar

METHOD

For the sponge, beat eggs and sugar until pale and fluffy, fold in flour. Line baking tray with silicon paper and spread the mix two centimetres thick and bake at 180C for 20 minutes until golden brown.

For the Marquise mix, melt chocolate over pan of boiling water. Dice butter and add to mix, stir until melted. In a separate bowl beat egg yolk and add to mix. Beat egg white to peak and add sugar. Fold egg white into chocolate mix and spread over cooled sponge. Set in the fridge.

THE GLASS HOUSE RESTAURANT

Rydal Road, Ambleside, Cumbria, LA22 9AN
Tel: 015394 32137, www.theglasshouserestaurant.co.uk

GOOD TASTE CAFÉ

THE
STUDIO

GOOD TASTE CAFÉ

Good Taste Café was set up by my wife Emma and I in May 2003. The café has built its reputation on the solid foundations of 'fresh is best' and 'use what's on your doorstep when it's available'.

We wanted to create an environment where people could enjoy great food and coffee, whether as part of a group or on their own, reading the paper and getting their daily fix of Good Taste relaxation. Here we use the principles of fine dining and cookery and apply them to everyday, accessible food to be enjoyed by all. We look forward to welcoming you to Good Taste.

The following recipes come from our other venture, The Studio Dining Room, which is tucked away off Station Street in Keswick.

The Studio Dining Room concept has been developed so that our customers can immerse themselves in a dining experience rather than simply booking a restaurant table.

Dinner is served in The Studio Kitchen, where a large dining table sits amid the action, letting you see exactly how our chefs produce your food to the highest standards. All is not what it seems, however, and our chefs are likely to have a little fun with your taste buds; expect the unexpected, and take a seat for a truly unique dining experience.

Peter Sidwell, proprietor

GOOD TASTE CAFÉ

Ham and eggs with brown sauce
Pressed ham hock terrine served with deep-fried poached egg and a brown sauce vinaigrette

Serves 4

INGREDIENTS

FOR THE TERRINE:

4 free range eggs

6 slices bread

sprig rosemary

2 eggs for egg wash

100g flour

3 x 1.2kg/2lb 12oz unsmoked ham hocks, on the bone

bouquet garni (2 bay leaves, few sprigs thyme, 2 sprigs parsley and few optional sprigs tarragon tied together)

1 tsp black peppercorns

2 shallots, chopped

1 bottle (75cl) dry white wine

4 tbsp white wine vinegar

2 tbsp small capers, rinsed and drained

50g/2oz gherkins, rinsed and chopped

generous handful parsley, finely chopped

salt and freshly ground black pepper

DRESSING:

50ml brown sauce

50ml sherry vinegar

50ml extra virgin olive oil

30ml water

METHOD

For terrine, put the ham hocks in a large stockpot and cover with cold water. Add bouquet garni, peppercorns and shallots. Pour in wine and vinegar, and add enough cold water to just cover ingredients. Bring to the boil, then simmer gently (no need to cover the pan) for a minimum of two hours or until the hocks are tender and the meat flakes easily. Leave hocks to cool in liquid for an hour. Remove hocks, cover with clingfilm and set aside. Discard trotters. Strain cooking liquid through a muslin-lined sieve into a clean pan. Place pan on a high heat and bring liquid to a rapid boil. Boil to reduce down to one pint, then pass it through a sieve into a jug. Peel skin off hocks, then shred meat into nuggets. Place in a large bowl with capers, gherkins and parsley. Mix well. Taste and season with pepper. Pile mixture into lined moulds and press down firmly. Slowly pour in reduced liquid, adding just enough to cover meat. As you pour, tap terrine dish on a hard surface to ensure liquid is spread throughout terrine. Cover with overhanging clingfilm and chill overnight. Boil six medium free-range eggs for three minutes and re-fresh in ice-cold water and leave to cool. In a food processor blend six slices of bread into crumbs, add a sprig of rosemary and a sprig of thyme. When eggs are cool, peel them and roll them in flour then egg wash then into the breadcrumbs. Cook breaded eggs in hot oil for one minute until golden. **For dressing,** add all the above ingredients into a bottle and shake until emulsified. **To serve,** place ham terrine in centre of plate, slice egg in half and place on top of terrine. Dress plate with salad leaves and salad dressing. Season egg with black pepper.

GOOD TASTE CAFÉ

19 Lake Road, Keswick, Cumbria, CA12 5BS
Tel: 017687 75973, www.simplygoodtaste.co.uk

GOOD TASTE CAFÉ

Roasted fillet of sea bass served with a wild mushroom and potato Lyonnaise and a salsa verde

Serves 4

INGREDIENTS

4 fillets sea bass

$^1/_2$ lemon

sea salt and pepper

1 tsp fennel seeds

50ml olive oil

SALSA VERDE:

1 handful parsley

1 tbsp capers

zest and juice of half lemon

50ml olive oil

$^1/_2$ garlic clove

2/3 anchovy fillets

POTATO LYONNAISE:

4 large potatoes

250g wild mushrooms

1 large white onion

rosemary

salt and pepper

vegetable stock

parsley

METHOD

Salsa verde, you can make this some time in advance. You can hand chop the ingredients on a board or use a food processor, but do not turn it on for too long. Chop the parsley, capers, anchovy fillets and garlic together. Scoop them into a bowl and stir in the lemon juice, olive oil and half a teaspoon of salt. **For potatoes Lyonnaise,** slice the onions finely and cook in a frying pan with a little olive oil until soft, turn the heat down and add the chopped rosemary, thyme, salt and pepper. Cook for a further 10/15 minutes. Remove onions from the pan, using the same pan return to the heat and add the sliced mushrooms, fry until golden, about five minutes. Add the mushrooms to the onions and stir together. Peel the potatoes and slice as thinly as possible, lay the sliced potatoes out in a baking dish so they cover the bottom of the dish, then add a layer of mushrooms and onions, then add another layer of potatoes, repeat process and finish with a neat layer of potatoes. Pour the stock over potatoes and cover with foil, cook for one hour at 180C. Remove foil after 40 minutes. To cook the fish heat a frying pan on a medium heat until very hot. Cut small slices into the sea bass fillets on the skin side so you are able to season the fish inside the cuts as well as on the outside. Season fillets with black pepper, sea salt and fennel seeds. Drizzle with olive oil on both sides, place the fish skin-side down into pan and hold the fillets down so that the skin does not curl up. Cook for 8-10 minutes in total, first one side then turn the fish over, and squeeze half a lemon into the pan and turn heat off. The residual heat in the pan will finish off cooking the sea bass, while you plate up the potatoes and salsa.

GOOD TASTE CAFÉ

19 Lake Road, Keswick, Cumbria, CA12 5BS
Tel: 017687 75973, www.simplygoodtaste.co.uk

GOOD TASTE CAFÉ

Lemon posset served with a ginger sable and a damson and blackberry sorbet

Serves 4

INGREDIENTS

1¹/₂ pints/852ml double cream

225g caster sugar

6 lemons

SORBET:

500g white sugar

400ml water

100ml damson gin

500g blackberries

juice of one lemon

GINGER SABLES:

250g butter

125g icing sugar

1 large egg yolk

325g plain flour

100g chopped candied ginger

¹/₂ tsp ground ginger

METHOD

To prepare, bring the sugar and cream to the boil and then simmer for one minute, then allow to cool. Add the juice of six lemons. Pour into dessert glasses. Place these into the fridge overnight, and in the morning the possets should be set.

Sorbet, place the sugar, water and gin into a large saucepan and place on a low heat to bring up to the boil. When the solution has come to the boil add the blackberries and the lemon juice. When the mixture has cooled blend with a hand blender and then pass through a sieve. Pour the mixture into an ice-cream machine and churn for 20 minutes or until frozen. If you don't have an ice-cream machine pour the mixture into a shallow tray and place it into the freezer, remembering to stir every 20 minutes or so to prevent it freezing into a block.

Ginger sable, in a mixing bowl add the softened butter, icing sugar and egg yolk and beat together to form a pale mixture. Add the ground ginger and flour and mix together, then add the candied ginger and mix together until it comes together. Turn the mixture out onto a clean work surface and shape into a long triangle, place in the fridge to firm up. Cut the biscuits into one centimetre thick slices and bake in the oven for 10 minutes at 160C.

GOOD TASTE CAFÉ

19 Lake Road, Keswick, Cumbria, CA12 5BS
Tel: 017687 75973, www.simplygoodtaste.co.uk

JERICHOS
AT WAVERLEY

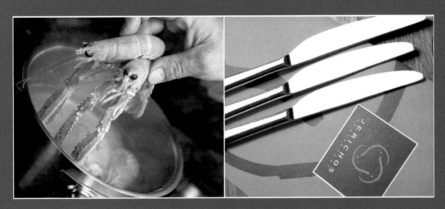

JERICHOS AT WAVERLEY

After twelve good years of business Jerichos has just relocated, moving 300 yards as the crow flies from Birch Street off Crescent Road to College Road, into one of the town's original hotels, becoming in the process a "restaurant with rooms".

Our newly-relocated and refurbished restaurant adds a welcome modern twist to Windermere and especially The Waverley, a lovely Victorian building, in the heart of the village, with a welcoming ambience that reflects the mood, atmosphere and quality that Jerichos stands for. Whether you are visiting the restaurant for dinner or joining us for breakfast, Chris' passion for food is replicated in each dish he serves. The evening a la carte menu guarantees that each dish is brimming with great tastes, using in-season quality produce, and with frequent changes there is always something different to try.

Jerichos at the Waverley is exactly the sort of place my wife Jo and I wanted to create, a fantastic modern restaurant serving great food within a great Victorian building, full of character and charm, with the additional option of bedrooms.

The menu is always big on taste and very concise in length guaranteeing freshly cooked real food every time. The marriage of good food and wine are important to us, so to complement the delicious food at Jerichos, we also have an extensive wine list giving you the opportunity to experience a global wealth of flavour, matched with food and our commitment to offering value for money. To make the choice easier try the 'Wines of the Month' or opt for our wine-tasting selection, a pre-chosen wine with each course.

Chris Blaydes

Asparagus and langoustine risotto
with deep-fried leek

Serves 6

INGREDIENTS

300g risotto rice

80ml olive oil

3 shallots, finely chopped

200ml white wine

800ml langoustine stock

18 whole langoustines

18 asparagus spears, 5cm in length

1 leek cut into julienne strips

tomato coulis (4 vine tomatoes,

60g butter, 2 tbsp olive oil, 2 tbsp

langoustine stock)

METHOD

For the tomato coulis, place the vine tomatoes into a pan with the butter, olive oil and langoustine stock, bring to the boil and simmer for five to ten minutes, liquidise the whole lot and pass through a fine sieve to remove all the seeds. Reserve for finishing the risotto. Place the whole langoustines, nine at a time into 900ml of boiling water, cook for two minutes, remove, peel and put the shells, all 18 back into the water, boil for 15 minutes, remove from the heat and leave to cool with the shells in. When cool pass through a sieve and reserve the stock, discard the shells. Blanch the asparagus spears in boiling salted water for three to four minutes until cooked but still firm to the bite, remove from the boiling water and place into a bowl of iced water to cool down quickly, remove when completely cool. Deep fry the leek (170C, 350F) until golden brown, remove from fryer onto kitchen paper to drain. Sweat the shallot in the olive oil until soft, about five minutes. Then add the rice and sweat for a minute or so longer. Add the white wine and reduce to a syrup. Add the stock little by little until all absorbed into the rice. Then add four tablespoons of tomato coulis, the langoustines, the asparagus and finally a knob of butter, very gently stir together and season to taste.

Serve immediately between six plates, making sure each person gets equal amounts of asparagus and langoustine, top with the deep-fried leek and garnish each plate with a tablespoon of tomato coulis drizzled around each serving.

JERICHOS AT WAVERLEY

College Road, Windermere, Cumbria, LA23 1BX
Tel: 015394 42522, www.jerichos.co.uk

JERICHOS AT WAVERLEY

Fillet of beef with French fries and garnish

Serves 6

INGREDIENTS

6 x 180g barrel trimmed beef fillet

6 x 8cm flat field mushrooms

6 x plum tomatoes cut in half lengthways

3 large washed Maris Piper potatoes

Dijon butter (1 tbsp Dijon mustard beaten with 120g salted butter)

red wine sauce

oil and butter for frying and grilling

METHOD

Method, do not peel the potatoes and cut into French fries along the length of the potatoes. Deep-fry at 170C for five to ten minutes to blanch the fries first. Remove from the heat and finish later.

In a hot frying pan add a knob of butter and one tablespoon of olive oil, season the fillets and adding three fillets at a time, being careful not to splash, colour well all over. Put to one side. To finish, clean pan and add another knob of butter and a tablespoon of oil, get the pan very hot and cook steaks evenly on both sides to your liking.

To finish the fries, drop back into the oil and fry until brown and crisp, turn out onto a kitchen paper lined tray to drain the oil and sprinkle with salt.

Season and grill the mushrooms and tomatoes, keep warm.

To assemble the dish place a mushroom in the centre of each plate and on either side of it half a tomato. Place a fillet on top of each mushroom followed by a knob of Dijon butter. Then pour your red wine sauce over and around each fillet. Finally, place a stack of fries on top of each fillet, just like a bonfire and serve immediately.

JERICHOS AT WAVERLEY

College Road, Windermere, Cumbria, LA23 1BX
Tel: 015394 42522, www.jerichos.co.uk

JERICHOS AT WAVERLEY

Vanilla panna cotta with shortbread and raspberries

Serves 6

INGREDIENTS

300ml full fat milk
300ml double cream
90g caster sugar
3$\frac{1}{2}$ gelatine leaves
$\frac{1}{2}$ split vanilla pod
1 large punnet fresh raspberries

SHORTBREAD ROUNDS X 12:

75g plain flour
75g self-raising flour
30g semolina
60g caster sugar
100g warm butter, not melted

RASPBERRY COULIS:

500g frozen raspberries, defrosted
500g caster sugar

RASPBERRY SORBET:

375g caster sugar
325ml water
60g liquid glucose
raspberry puree left over from above

METHOD

Method, place gelatine leaves in bowl of cold water and leave to soften for five to ten minutes. Cut vanilla pod in half length-ways, scrape out seeds. Place a saucepan with vanilla pods, sugar, cream and milk over medium heat and slowly bring to boil. Remove from heat and leave to stand for five to ten minutes. Bring cream back to boil then remove from heat. Drain gelatine leaves. Add to hot cream, stir well and make sure all gelatine dissolved. Strain and pour into six dariole moulds, allow to cool, and cover with cling-film, chill for eight hours. **For shortbread,** pre-heat oven to gas mark 2/300F/150C. Place all ingredients in food mixer or bowl and, using biscuit beater or hands, bring all together to form soft ball of dough. Gently roll out to a thickness of 4mm and using a 6cm biscuit cutter, cut out biscuits. Transfer to non-stick baking tray and bake for 20-25 minutes. When cool, place in airtight container. **For coulis,** sprinkle sugar over defrosted raspberries and leave to one side for two hours. Liquidise and pass whole lot through fine sieve into jug to remove seeds. Reserve six tablespoons of this puree to decorate plate, the rest will be used for raspberry sorbet. **For sorbet,** in a saucepan, bring sugar, water and glucose to boil, stirring occasionally. Boil for three to four minutes, if you have a saccharometer the reading should be 30 Beaume or 1.26 density. Strain syrup through metal sieve, leave to cool. Place puree into saucepan with sorbet syrup and bring to boil, simmer for five minutes, remove from heat and cool, then chill for two hours. Pour chilled mixture into ice-cream maker and churn for 15-20 minutes until semi-firm. Place in freezer until ready to use.
To assemble, place biscuit in middle of each plate, on top of this a layer of raspberries and then another biscuit. Place panna cotta on top of this followed by ball of raspberry sorbet, making a tower. Around each drizzle a tablespoon of raspberry coulis. Dust with icing sugar.

JERICHOS AT WAVERLEY

College Road, Windermere, Cumbria, LA23 1BX
Tel: 015394 42522, www.jerichos.co.uk

LUCYCOOKS

...and so can you!

...er you're 9 or 90, we offer a whole
...vidual one day practical courses
...ns designed to suit everyone
...e to Nigella!

...all entertained!

LUCYCOOKS

LucyCooks must be one of the most scenic locations for a cookery school in the UK. Its position in the Lake District National Park and at the heart of Staveley's Mill Yard surrounded not only by stunning scenery, but also by an eclectic group of artisan businesses, has made it a destination for both budding cooks and those seeking an alternative to restaurant dining. The LucyCooks demo and dine is now a well-established favourite with locals and visitors alike. Rather like a 'culinary book club' without the homework, the evening commences with a drink and a chance to meet up with the other guests. There is then an opportunity to take a quick look around our purpose-built cookery school before the evening starts in earnest. Guests are seated 'dinner party' style in our lovely big Aga kitchen adjoining the River Kent and enjoy watching our chef demonstrate something delicious, upon which they then dine! Recipes and handy hints will be distributed and there will be the opportunity to ask questions. We run at least four demo and dine evenings per month and a typical selection includes 'A Taste of Cumbria,' 'Mediterranean Medley' and 'A Taste of the Orient.' Descriptions are available on our website or call us.

As you would expect we also offer a wide range of day and half-day practical courses as well as bespoke events, children's courses and team-based challenges. Check our website for details, www.lucycooks.co.uk

Lucy Nicholson

LUCYCOOKS

Timbale of hot smoked salmon bound together
with crème fraiche, spring onions and red peppers,
served with rocket leaves and tomato concasse

Serves 4

INGREDIENTS

16oz/400g hot smoked salmon

3oz/75g crème fraiche

¹/₂ red pepper, diced

2 spring onions, diced

salt and pepper

2 vine tomatoes

2oz/50g rocket leaves

4 lemon wedges

METHOD

Method, in a large bowl, flake the smoked salmon. Then add the crème fraiche, pepper and spring onions, mix well and adjust the seasoning.
For the concasse, cut a small cross in the bottom of the tomatoes and place in a pan of boiling water for 30 seconds, drain off the water and cool in iced water for two minutes. Quarter, de-seed and dice the tomatoes.

To serve, divide the rocket leaves between the four plates and place them in the centre. Using a large scone cutter, place onto the rocket then fill with half of the mixture, do the same with the remaining three plates. Then scatter the tomato concasse around the salmon. Serve with the lemon wedges.

LUCYCOOKS

Mill Yard, Staveley, Kendal, Cumbria, LA8 9LR
Tel: 015394 32288, www.lucycooks.co.uk

LUCYCOOKS

Roasted Lakeland lamb rump steak studded with rosemary carved over sweet potato mash with root vegetables and a red wine jus

Serves 4

INGREDIENTS

LAMB:
4 lamb steaks
24 sprigs rosemary
2 tbsp olive oil
pinch salt and pepper

SWEET POTATO MASH:
2 large sweet potatoes
50g/2oz butter
pinch salt and pepper

ROAST ROOT VEGETABLES:
1 carrot
1/2 swede
1 parsnip
1/2 celeriac

4 leaves fresh wild garlic, shredded
or 2 cloves garlic, crushed
2 tbsp olive oil
pinch salt and pepper

RED WINE JUS:
3kg/6¹/₂lbs lamb bones
2kg/4¹/₂lbs mixed vegetables – carrots,
celery, onions, tomatoes, parsnips, leeks,
fennel (all roughly chopped)
100g/4oz tomato pureé
¹/₂ litre red wine
2 sprigs rosemary or thyme
8 litres water
2 tbsp olive oil

METHOD

To prepare, peel and roughly chop all roast root vegetables. Preheat oven to 180C/350F/Gas mark 4. First start the stock for the jus by rubbing the tomato puree onto the bones and place in a roasting tin in the oven for 30-40 minutes until browned. Now pour the oil into a 20-litre stock pot, heat up, add the vegetables and brown. Next, add the bones and pour over the water and bring to the boil, continue to boil for six hours skimming off any fat floating on the top as required.

Remove the bones and vegetables and continue to boil, add the wine and herbs and boil until the jus thickens (just enough to coat the back of a spoon).

Next, season the lamb and make six small cuts in the fat about 2cm deep and push rosemary into each cut so that a little is just poking out of the top. Heat up the oil in a large non-stick frying pan and seal the lamb rump steaks on all sides then transfer to a roasting tin and place in the oven for 20-25 minutes. Peel and roughly chop the sweet potatoes and put into a large pan and cover with salted water. Bring to the boil and cook until tender, drain, add the butter, mash and adjust seasoning. **Place** the roughly chopped vegetables in a roasting tin and the oil, salt and pepper, mix well and roast for 20-30 minutes. **To serve,** put a spoonful of the mash in the centre of each plate. Carve the lamb and place on top of the mash and put the vegetables to the side, then pour over a little of the jus. *Picture shows a trio of lamb. Please see our website, below, for details of loin and roasted rack of lamb recipes.*

LUCYCOOKS

Mill Yard, Staveley, Kendal, Cumbria, LA8 9LR
Tel: 015394 32288, www.lucycooks.co.uk

LUCYCOOKS

Baked chocolate cake served with fresh summer berries and sour cream

Serves 6

INGREDIENTS

600g/21¹/₂ oz plain chocolate (70pc cocoa solids)

400g/13¹/₂ oz butter

4 large eggs

120g/4oz caster sugar

sour cream

selection of summer fruits (strawberries, redcurrants, blackcurrants)

METHOD

To prepare, pre-heat oven to 170C/325F/gas 3. Break the chocolate into pieces and put them in the saucepan. Add the butter and melt gently over a very low heat, stirring occasionally, until melted and smooth. Let it cool.

Put the eggs and sugar in a large bowl and beat with a hand-held electric mixer until trebled in volume. Add one quarter of the melted chocolate mixture into the bowl and, using a plastic spatula, mix gently until thoroughly incorporated. Add the remaining melted chocolate and fold in gently until well mixed.

Pour the mixture into the prepared tin and bake in a preheated oven at 170C for eight minutes. The cake will be slightly soft to touch, not firm. Don't be tempted to cook it for any longer than this. Remove from the oven and let cool in the tin. Serve with the selection of summer fruits and a dollop of soured cream.

MORREL'S RESTAURANT

MORREL'S RESTAURANT

Our partnership was created 16 years ago, comprising myself and my wife Rebecca, her brother Errol, and his wife Carol. We have run several businesses since then, but have always wanted a 'proper' restaurant. Our dreams came true in 2000 when we purchased a small hotel and created Morrel's.

Errol and Carol take care of the service in our modern 50-cover restaurant, whilst I, along with my head chef David Lamont, run the kitchen.

Our ethos is simple, fresh ingredients cooked with care and passion. The surrounding beauty of the area inspires us on a daily basis, even the rain!

All our suppliers are local businesses who go that extra mile to deliver fresh produce daily, meat is locally sourced and all poultry and eggs are free range.

Our main a la carte menu changes with the seasons, and our Sunday table d'hote features local beef with proper gravy.

The growing number of vegetarians are also imaginatively catered for with plenty to choose from. Morrel's truly is a labour of love for all concerned.

Karl Link, chef proprietor

MORREL'S RESTAURANT

Seared White Gold sea scallops and chorizo with pineapple and mango relish

Serves 4

12 king scallops	**FOR THE RELISH:**
100g chorizo	150g pineapple
15g chard	100g mango
15g rocket	1 red chilli
olive oil	25g red pepper (julienne)
butter	1 red onion
seasoning	25g blanched raisins
	1 tbsp chopped mint
	I tbsp chopped coriander
	1 lime
	seasoning

Method, slice the pineapple and mango and place under a grill to lightly brown. Once cool finely dice and place into a bowl, add the finely diced red onion, chilli (seeds removed), julienne of red pepper, blanched raisins, zest and juice of lime and the chopped herbs. Mix together and season. Refrigerate for 24 hours to allow the juices to come out.

To serve, place the relish in a small ring and top with rocket and chard. Pan sear the seasoned scallops and chorizo in oil and a little butter for 45 seconds each side until golden brown. Place alternate around the plate, spoon over the oil from the pan.

MORREL'S RESTAURANT

34 Lake Road, Keswick, Cumbria, CA12 5DQ
Tel: 017687 72666, www.morrels.co.uk

MORREL'S RESTAURANT

Grass-reared Cumbrian pork three ways with parsnip & apple puree, black mash & crushed garden peas

Serves 4

INGREDIENTS

250g pork belly
4 Cumberland sausages
250g pork fillet
1 onion
1 carrot
1 clove garlic
honey

PUREE:

2 parsnips
1 onion
1 large Granny Smith
20g butter
1 tbsp double cream
seasoning

BLACK MASH:

2 large potatoes
50g black pudding
butter
seasoning
fried onions

CRUSHED GARDEN PEAS:

100g garden peas
sage leaf
seasoning

METHOD

For puree, place chopped parsnip and onion in a pan, gently sweat, cover with water and cook until soft, add the chopped skinned apples and cook for a further two minutes. Strain off liquid and place in a blender with butter, cream and seasoning until a smooth consistency. **For mash,** make the mash potato. Fry off chopped black pudding in a pan with a little butter for a few minutes. Mix into mash, check seasoning. **For peas,** blanch defrosted peas into boiling water for 30 seconds. Refresh. Using a fork crush peas. Finely chop sage leaf and add to peas and season. **For pork belly,** trim any excess fat, roll and tie firmly with butcher's string. Sweat off chopped onion, carrot and garlic, add pork belly and brown, place in oven at 130C for one hour 15 minutes. Remove and leave to rest. **Method,** place sausages in pan with a little oil and brown evenly. Cut pork fillet into one inch pieces and place in pan with sausages, colour for 30 seconds each side then place in oven for five minutes at 200C. While this is cooking fry off onions and make sauce. Remove pork belly from tray, add 500ml of pork stock and reduce by half, strain through a sieve into a pan and reduce further until consistency coats back of a spoon, check seasoning.
To serve, cut belly into four pieces, remove string, place in a pan, brush with honey and glaze. Place warmed up black mash in a ring to shape, slice sausage on an angle and place on top, spoon over fried onions. Shape warmed puree with two dessert spoons and sit on pork belly. Do same with peas for pork fillet using two teaspoons. Pour sauce around plate.

MORREL'S RESTAURANT

34 Lake Road, Keswick, Cumbria, CA12 5DQ
Tel: 017687 72666, www.morrels.co.uk

MORREL'S RESTAURANT

White chocolate cheesecake with toffee and raspberries

Serves 4

INGREDIENTS

6 digestive biscuits	15g caster sugar
50g butter	250ml double cream
150g white chocolate callets	80g fresh raspberries
100g cream cheese	1 tin condensed milk

METHOD

For the cheesecake, melt the butter and add to the crushed biscuits, place into four ring moulds and leave in fridge. Boil the cream and sugar, add the chocolate and whisk into the cream. Add the cream cheese and blitz until smooth. Allow to cool then pour into rings and refrigerate until set. **For the toffee,** boil the tin of condensed milk in a pan of boiling water for three to four hours then allow to cool completely. **For the raspberries,** place two tablespoons of water and one tablespoon of sugar in a pan with a few raspberries and reduce to a syrup. Push through a sieve to remove pips, allow to cool.

To serve, remove the cheesecake from the rings using a hot knife or blow torch, place in the centre of the plate, arrange the raspberries around the cheesecake, pour over the syrup. Place toffee on top using two teaspoons to shape. Decorate with chocolate.

MORREL'S RESTAURANT

34 Lake Road, Keswick, Cumbria, CA12 5DQ
Tel: 017687 72666, www.morrels.co.uk

NO 10 RESTAURANT

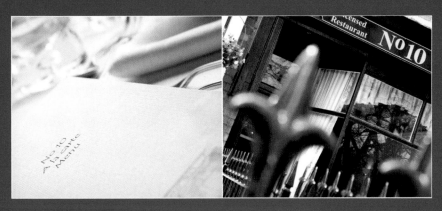

No 10 RESTAURANT

No 10 has been established for over 17 years but Paul and Sarah Minett have owned the restaurant for just over two years. The 24 covers in the restaurant are set in an old Victorian house dating back to the 18th Century on the busy Scotland road in the Cumbrian town of Carlisle. Paul and Sarah started their catering career over 20 years ago in hotels in the south of England. Sarah took a break from catering to raise children whilst Paul progressed through the kitchen at Center Parcs in Norfolk to the role of sous chef of 13 restaurants.

Paul moved to Newmarket race course to become head chef then moving on into Buckinghamshire to the home of British motor sport at Silverstone, taking control of the 2001 Grand Prix producing 42,000 meals over the weekend with his team.

Paul moved to London after that to become head chef of private catering for Sodexho in the City of London, working at such places as Buckingham Palace garden parties, Chelsea Flower Show, Royal Ascot, Lords cricket ground, British Open golf and PGA golf in Spain as part of his daily role. Fancying a change of scenery and pace of life, Paul moved his family to Cumbria to run Center Parcs at Whinfell Forest in Penrith as executive chef for four years before deciding that it was time to run his own business. Paul and Sarah purchased No 10 which has a great reputation in Carlisle and outlying areas for producing locally-sourced produce cooked to perfection in an intimate, relaxed environment. Paul and Sarah also provide catering for small to medium-sized events in marquees for weddings and private functions.

Paul Minett, owner

No 10 RESTAURANT

Seared Solway king scallops on mint and pea puree with aged balsamic vinegar

Serves 2

INGREDIENTS

8 large king Solway scallops	1 tsp reduced or aged balsamic vinegar
100ml whipping or double cream	pinch salt
100g frozen garden peas	pinch white ground pepper
4 fresh mint leaves	5ml olive oil

METHOD

Method, place the garden peas and cream in a pan and bring to boil for a few seconds, remove from the heat and allow to cool for 10 minutes. Add the four mint leaves and puree with a hand blender until the mixture is a smooth green puree (a paste that is not too runny but not one lump). Add a small pinch of salt and pepper to taste. If balsamic is not sticky place in a pan and put on a heat and allow to boil and reduce to a sticky consistency. Once it is sticky allow to cool slightly. Place a medium-sized flat frying pan on the heat, and while the pan is heating up make sure that the scallops are clean by removing any brown lines or large lumps on brown areas. Add olive oil to the pan allowing the oil to heat. Just as the oil starts to smoke, place the scallops flesh-side down. Allow the scallops to seal on this side for about one to two minutes, sprinkling with a small pinch of salt and pepper as they are cooking. After this time you will see the scallops turning golden brown. Turn them over. Again, sprinkle the scallops with a small pinch of salt and pepper.

To serve, start plating up the dish by spooning a line of pea mixture onto the plate and place four king scallops on the pea mixtures. Using a spoon drizzle the reduced balsamic mixture over the scallops and present.

No 10 RESTAURANT

Eden Mount, Carlisle, Cumbria, CA3 9LY
Tel: 01228 524183, www.no10limited.co.uk

No 10 RESTAURANT

Eden fillet of beef with wild mushrooms and red wine sauce

Serves 1

INGREDIENTS

1 x 8oz/225g fillet of beef trimmed and ready to use

70g wild mushrooms

100ml chicken or beef stock

100ml red wine

5ml olive oil

2 pinches salt and pepper

METHOD

Method, place the red wine in a pan and place on the heat, then reduce by half, then add the chicken or beef stock and reduce the whole liquid by 80pc. This will produce a strong red wine flavoured sauce that is of a slightly thicker consistency. Add salt and pepper to taste. With the wild mushrooms remove any dirt and twigs. Don't wash in water as this will affect the flavour and texture of the mushrooms. Place a flat-bottomed pan on a high heat, and as the pan heats up add the olive oil and when the oil just starts to smoke add the fillet steak flat-side first. Sprinkle with salt and pepper, turn the steak over so that all sides are golden brown all over and again sprinkle sides that have just been sealed with salt and pepper. Place on a small flat baking tray and place in the oven on 200-220C or gas mark 5 and cook to your liking. Place a pan on the heat with a small amount of oil in it and allow this to heat up. When the oil is hot add the mushrooms, and make sure that the mushrooms are moved around every 15-20 seconds so they cook evenly and don't burn. Once the mushrooms are cooked sprinkle with salt and pepper and remove from the heat. Take the fillet steak out of the oven when cooked to your liking and allow to rest for about one to two minutes.

To serve, place the red wine sauce on the plate, making a small pool, and place fillet steak in the centre of the pool. On top of this spoon the cooked wild mushrooms and present.

No 10 RESTAURANT

Eden Mount, Carlisle, Cumbria, CA3 9LY
Tel: 01228 524183, www.no10limited.co.uk

No 10 RESTAURANT

Burnt lemon tart with crème fraiche and Kirsch black cherries

Serves 6-8

INGREDIENTS

PASTRY:

225g plain flour

pinch salt

150g salted butter

75g caster or icing sugar

1 whole egg

1 egg yolk

FILLING:

4 lemons

4 whole eggs

75g caster sugar

100ml double or whipping cream

TOPPING & FINISHING:

20g brown sugar

10g thick set crème fraiche

4 per portion, pitted black cherries
marinated in Kirsch

Method, make the pastry by sifting the flour with the salt. Rub in the butter until the mixture resembles crumbs. Now stir in the sugar. Add the egg yolk with the whole egg. Work everything together and refrigerate for 30-60 minutes before using. Roll out the pastry and line an eight-inch pastry case and allow to rest for 10 minutes. Cover with greaseproof paper and add baking beans and place in a pre-heated oven at 200C/400F/gas mark 6 until the pastry is cooked and looking lightly golden brown. Mix the whole eggs, cream and sugar in a bowl and blend until a smooth mixture. Grate the outside zest of the lemon, not grating the white of the lemon just the yellow flesh, then add this to the egg and cream mixture. Juice the four lemons and add the lemon to the mixture, then mix all together as this will set if not mixed.

Pour the egg/cream and lemon mixture into the pastry case and cook in a pre-heated oven at 140C/320F/gas mark 3 until the mixture has set. Don't allow the mixture to brown or boil as this will split the tart. Once cooked allow to cool then refrigerate until cooled.

To serve, cut the tart into six or eight (if you like larger portions cut into six). Sprinkle with a light covering of brown sugar and burn with a gas gun, caramelising the sugar until golden brown not burnt. Place on the plate and add a spoon of thick crème fraiche and finish with four marinated black cherries.

No 10 RESTAURANT

Eden Mount, Carlisle, Cumbria, CA3 9LY
Tel: 01228 524183, www.no10limited.co.uk

THE PHEASANT

THE PHEASANT

Game in season, the freshest of local produce, wonderful surroundings and a unique atmosphere are but some of the attributes that customers of The Pheasant at Bassenthwaite tell their friends about. This 15th Century inn, with its timeless elegance and understated luxury, has every modern comfort for its local, national and international clientele. Situated in the quieter Northern part of the Lake District it is in a beautiful rural location within easy reach of the M6, the Midlands and Scotland.

Gleaming silver cutlery and shining crystal glassware on crisp white napery greets guests in the beamed dining room. The relaxed atmosphere with the friendly professional service is the hallmark of this delightful and cheery restaurant. Lighter lunches are served in the lounges and the renowned and award-winning bar. In summer months the magnificent gardens can be enjoyed while nibbling on a plate of organic smoked salmon and quaffing a glass of ice-cold Chablis.

Often described as the epitome of a traditional inn, The Pheasant is extremely comfortable and welcoming, and has a warm and friendly character with an abundance of atmosphere.

Matthew Wylie, managing director

THE PHEASANT

Seared hand-dived scallops with local black pudding, butternut squash puree and pickled carrot and fennel salad

Serves 1

INGREDIENTS

SCALLOPS:
3 large, fresh king scallops
(hand-dived if possible)
1 tsp olive oil
1/2 lemon
pinch sea salt

BUTTERNUT SQUASH PUREE:
1 butternut squash
50g unsalted butter

BLACK PUDDING:
2 x 2cm thick slice black pudding
1 tsp olive oil

CARROT AND FENNEL SALAD:
1 carrot
1 bulb fennel
2 tbsp white wine vinegar
2 tbsp icing sugar

METHOD

For the pickled carrot and fennel salad, peel carrot into ribbons. Finely slice the fennel. Place all ingredients in a bowl and mix thoroughly. Season to taste.

For the butternut squash puree, peel squash. Cut into pieces. Oven roast until soft. Puree the squash whilst hot with the butter using a stick blender or similar, until smooth. Season to taste.

For black pudding, cut circles out of the slice of black pudding using a 4cm round pastry ring. Heat oil in pan and fry black pudding for two minutes each side until crisp.

For the scallops, remove coral (orange-coloured 'tail') and muscle (clear membrane around the scallop). Pat dry. Heat frying pan over a high heat. Add oil. Place scallops in the pan and cook for 45 seconds on each side (or until coloured on both sides). Season with lemon juice and sea salt to taste.

To Serve, arrange black pudding circles neatly on the plate, add a layer of the puree and then perch the scallops on top. Garnish with the salad and serve.

THE PHEASANT

Bassenthwaite Lake, Nr Cockermouth, Cumbria, CA13 9YE
Tel: 017687 76234, www.the-pheasant.co.uk

THE PHEASANT

Pan-fried pave of halibut with grilled langoustine, julienne of vegetables and a white wine, butter and shallot sauce

Serves 1

INGREDIENTS

1 medium fresh langoustine (live if possible)

6oz/170g fillet of halibut with skin on

1 tsp olive oil

JULIENNE OF VEGETABLES:

1 carrot

1 leek (white part only)

1 courgette

1 red pepper

SHALLOT SAUCE:

$\frac{1}{4}$ cup white wine vinegar

$\frac{1}{4}$ cup dry white wine

1 shallot

225g cold butter

METHOD

Preparation, cut vegetables into long thin batons. Bring saucepan of salted water to the boil. Add carrots and boil for two minutes. Remove and reserve. Add rest of vegetables and boil for one minute. Reserve. Split langoustine lengthways. De-vein. Season lightly with sea salt and lemon juice, brush with a little melted butter. Place under grill until cooked – about 45 seconds. Pat halibut dry and season with salt and pepper. Put oil in a non-stick skillet over a moderate heat until hot but not smoking. Cook halibut for about three to five minutes each side, turn once. Should be golden brown on both sides.

Method, finely chop the shallot. Add shallot, vinegar and wine to a saucepan and simmer over a medium low heat. Reduce by half. Chop butter into eight pieces. Change to a low heat, add butter one piece at a time and whisk vigorously. When first is incorporated add second and so on. Be patient and don't add too much butter at any one time. Sauce should be thick and creamy. Season to taste. Use immediately to avoid splitting.

To serve, cream some potato. Place in the centre of plate. Place halibut on and then top with sauce. Add vegetable garnish and then langoustine, serve with a small herb cress salad.

THE PHEASANT

Bassenthwaite Lake, Nr Cockermouth, Cumbria, CA13 9YE
Tel: 017687 76234, www.the-pheasant.co.uk

THE PHEASANT

Dark chocolate mousse with damsons in gin

Serves 1

INGREDIENTS

340g dark chocolate	**DAMSON GIN SMOOTHIE:**
2 tbsp sugar	damson gin (pre-made)
2 large eggs, separated	damson jam
50g cocoa powder	1 cup low fat plain yoghurt
4 tsp brandy or rum (optional)	2 cups of ice

METHOD

To make mousse, melt chocolate and allow to cool. Mix in the cocoa powder. Beat egg yolks and whisk into mixture. Add two tablespoons of water and beat into the chocolate until fully blended. Whisk egg whites until soft peaks form with the sugar and fold carefully into chocolate mixture. Place damson in centre of tear drop (remove stone). Allow mixture to set until piping consistency and pipe into chocolate tear.

For damson gin smoothie, blend all ingredients together.

THE PHEASANT

Bassenthwaite Lake, Nr Cockermouth, Cumbria, CA13 9YE
Tel: 017687 76234, www.the-pheasant.co.uk

PUNCH BOWL INN

PUNCH BOWL INN

The Punch Bowl Inn nestles snugly 'amongst the damsons,' in the delightfully unspoilt Lyth Valley at Crosthwaite. With the village church of St Mary's right next door, the rural charm of bell ringing and bird song combined with uninterrupted views down the valley make this a stunning location. After a complete refurbishment the present-day inn is a blend of log fire comfort and homeliness, old charm and new luxury, which provides a relaxed mixture of excellent food, comfortable interiors, good beers and wines.

The nine bedrooms are decorated individually with hand-picked cushions and throws, flat-screen TVs, and smart bathrooms with free-standing roll-top baths. The biggest and the best is Noble, occupying the whole of the third floor, and open to the eaves throughout.

With two different eating areas to choose from, the same menu is served throughout.

The restaurant is light and airy, with polished oak floorboards and comfortable leather chairs.

The bar area is warm and friendly, with a Brathay slate bar top, antique furniture and open fires.

Chalkboards reveal the seasonal menu, wines and Champagnes by the glass and foreign draught and bottled beers alongside a range of local hand-pulled real ales.

The food here concentrates on the best of fresh local produce, with a good portion of imagination. Local specialities and pub favourites sit alongside more elegant delicacies. It's worth noting that they have been awarded regional dining pub of the year 2008, by the Good Pub Guide, Michelin Pub guide, and also Lake District Life Magazine's Restaurant of the year 2007/2008.

The Punch Bowl is definitely a Lakeland inn worth a visit. Whatever you are looking for, good food, luxurious rooms, peace and relaxation or good walking territory, this is the place.

Paul Spencer and Richard Rose

PUNCH BOWL INN

Crab ravioli

Serves 4-6

INGREDIENTS

PASTA:

500g pasta flour

25ml olive oil

50ml water

2 medium free range eggs

pinch table salt

8 medium free range egg yolks

SALMON AND CRAB FILLING:

500g salmon

salt and cayenne pepper

250g brown crab

250ml cream

250g white crab

chopped chives

2 eggs

zest of one lemon

CRAB OIL:

shell of crab

chopped chive

1 tbsp tomato paste

tomato concasse

500ml olive oil

mirepoix (1 carrot, green leek,

1 onion, 1 celery)

brandy

METHOD

For the pasta, in a food processor, add the flour and salt. In a measuring jug add the yolks, water and oil, whisk together. Turn the food processor on, and mix the flour and salt, slowly adding the yolk mixture. Let the mixture turn into crumbs, then turn the processor off and work the mixture into a paste by hand. Let the paste rest for 30 minutes before rolling. **For salmon and crab filling,** blitz salmon and brown crab in a food processor with a pinch of salt, for one to two minutes. Scrape the sides with a spatula and add one whole egg and one egg white, then blitz for a further 30 seconds. Add cream and blitz for ten seconds. Scrape out of the bowl and pass through a sieve, into a mixing bowl. Fold in the white crab, the lemon zest and the chives and season. **For crab oil,** roast the crab with the tomato paste and mirepoix for 30 minutes at 180C. Take out of the oven and place in a heavy-bottomed boiling pan. De-glaze with the brandy, then add oil and warm slightly. Leave to infuse for 30 minutes, then pass through a muslin cloth, and finish with the tomato concasse and chopped chive. **For ravioli,** roll out pasta on a machine or by hand. Using a pastry cutter, cut out discs to a size of your choice (two needed for one ravioli). Place a spoonful of mixture into the centre of one disc, then brush edges with water to help layers of pasta stick together. Gently place a second disc on top, nipping the edges together all the way round, making sure no air is trapped. Bring a pan of salted water to the boil. Add ravioli and cook for five minutes. Serve with wilted spinach and the crab oil.

PUNCH BOWL INN

Crosthwaite, Lyth Valley, Cumbria, LA8 8HR
Tel: 015395 68237, www.the-punchbowl.co.uk

PUNCH BOWL INN

Lakeland lamb with creamed leeks and duck fat potatoes

Serves 4-6

INGREDIENTS

200g spring lamb loin

200g lamb shoulder steak, (braised and picked)

1 leek

2 large Maris Piper potatoes

100ml double cream

4 sprigs rosemary

4 cloves garlic

100g butter

duck fat

beef stock

salt and pepper

mirepoix (1 carrot, green of leek, 1 onion, 1 celery)

METHOD

For creamed leeks, reduce the double cream down until it turns yellow and thickens. Whilst the cream is reducing, blanch the sliced leek in some boiling water for 30 seconds, then refresh in iced water. Wring out the leeks in a tea towel or salad spinner, and pat dry. Add the leeks to the cream and season to taste.

For duck fat potatoes, peel potatoes, then cut into one-inch cubes, giving three potatoes per portion. Cover potatoes with the duck fat in a heavy-bottomed pan or roasting tray and gently cook until soft (approximately 30-40 minutes) Remove potatoes from duck fat and leave to cool on a resting wire. To reheat, colour each side in a heavy-bottomed frying pan, then place in oven for four minutes.

For mashed potato, cover the potato trimmings from the cubes in salted cold water. Bring to a simmer and gently cook until soft; then drain and leave to steam dry for five minutes. Put them through a potato ricer, add butter and season to taste.

For lamb shoulder, cover the shoulder steaks in beef stock, chopped vegetables, garlic and thyme. Cover with tin foil and cook for two hours at 180C or until meat is soft and tender. Remove from stock; allow to cool, and flaking meat down discard any fat. Add to pre-made pastry case and pipe mash on top.
Place the stock in the fridge to set.

For lamb loin, season the lamb on a tray. In a small oven-proof frying pan, add the butter and heat until melted and foaming. Seal the lamb in butter and add two sprigs of rosemary and two cloves of garlic. Cook in the oven for two minutes at 180C. Roll over and cook for a further two minutes. Remove from oven and leave somewhere warm to rest for two minutes. Slice to serve.

PUNCH BOWL INN

Crosthwaite, Lyth Valley, Cumbria, LA8 8HR
Tel: 015395 68237, www.the-punchbowl.co.uk

PUNCH BOWL INN

Apple tart tatin with damson ice cream

Serves 4-6

INGREDIENTS

ICE-CREAM:

250g damson jam

500ml milk

500ml cream

10 egg yolks

150g sugar

TATIN:

100g butter

100g sugar

pinch cinnamon

2 Golden Delicious apples

200g puff pastry

METHOD

For the ice-cream, warm the milk and cream until almost boiling, then remove from heat. Make a paste with yolks and sugar, and beat with a whisk, or in a mixer, until pale and fluffy. Add the milk and cream to the yolk paste slowly, and be careful not to split the egg mix. Return to the heat and cook mixture until thick, and coats the back of a spoon (71C) Churn the mixture in an ice-cream machine, or place in a freezer, and stir every 30 minutes until set.

For the tatin, cream butter, sugar and cinnamon together to make a pale yellow paste. Peel and core the apples, and cut them into halves. In a heavy-bottomed pan, make half a centimetre layer of butter paste. Arrange the apples in the pan. Roll out puff pastry big enough to cover the pan, and lay the pastry over the apples; folding in the edges to keep the apples enclosed. Make a small hole in the middle of the pastry. Place the pan on a high heat until the sugar and butter paste turns to caramel, and starts to bubble. Cook in the over for 10 minutes or until the puff pastry is golden at 180C. Remove from oven and turn out onto a tray immediately. Serve with ice-cream.

PUNCH BOWL INN

Crosthwaite, Lyth Valley, Cumbria, LA8 8HR
Tel: 015395 68237, www.the-punchbowl.co.uk

QUINCE & MEDLAR

QUINCE & MEDLAR
RESTAURANT

QUINCE & MEDLAR

Quince and Medlar is the home of Colin and Louisa Le Voi and their young family.
Colin and Louisa, both Cumbrian-born and raised, moved into the restaurant in a listed
building next to Cockermouth Castle in January 1989, after gaining valuable experience and
inspiration working at Sharrow Bay hotel on Ullswater under the watchful eyes of the late
Francis Coulson and Brian Sack.

The unique, intimate dining room is packed with character and charm. Interesting paintings
adorn the walls by well-respected Cumbrian artists.

Beautifully imaginative vegetarian dishes to delight all food lovers, using seasonal ingredients,
are passionately prepared with artistic flair and style by Colin and Louisa along with their
friendly personal service. They have gained many awards over the years and non-vegetarians
certainly don't miss the meat.

Cockermouth is a Georgian market town on the edge of the Lake District, where William
Wordsworth was born in 1770, and has recently received Cittaslow status; this means it is now
part of a network of towns where quality of life is important. The Cittaslow movement
celebrates and promotes tradition, quality and service, which follows in the line of what Quince
and Medlar is about.

The wine list is entirely organic, and the beers. Interesting fruit juices and cordials are also on
offer to complement the food.

Colin and Louisa Le Voi

QUINCE & MEDLAR

Roasted fennel, leek and Allerdale goat's cheese filo tart

Serves 4

INGREDIENTS

8 sheets filo pastry

2 medium bulbs fennel, quartered

2 medium leeks, sliced,

small knob butter, melted

1 tbsp whipping cream

100g Allerdale goat's cheese, grated

4 tsp creme fraiche

parsley, chopped

salt and ground pepper

olive oil

METHOD

Method, pre-heat oven to gas 6/200C/400F. Grease four six-centimetre loose-bottomed tartlet tins with olive oil. Cut filo pastry sheets in half. Criss-cross four sheets in each tin and press down to form a pastry nest. Brush with a little melted butter. Bake for about ten minutes until golden brown. Allow to cool and take out of tin. Blanch fennel in salted boiling water for about three minutes, drain and drizzle with olive oil, salt and pepper on an oven tray and roast for about eight minutes. Cook leeks with a knob of butter for about two minutes, add whipping cream, and simmer for five minutes and season. Pour leek mixture into filo cases with two quarters of fennel on top of each. Put a dollop of creme fraiche and a sprinkling of goat's cheese on each tartlet and bake for 10-15 minutes until golden.

QUINCE & MEDLAR

13 Castlegate, Cockermouth, Cumbria, CA13 9EU
Tel: 01900 823579, www.quinceandmedlar.co.uk

QUINCE & MEDLAR

Baked aubergine with chickpea and apricot pate and strips of char-grilled sweet red pepper

Serves 4

INGREDIENTS

AUBERGINE:

3-4 medium aubergines, sliced 1cm thick (allow 6 slices per person)

1 tsp ground cumin

1 tsp ground paprika

1 tbsp olive oil

2 tbsp tomato puree

Salt and ground pepper

TOMATO RELISH:

4 large tomatoes, skinned and chopped

1 medium onion, sliced

drizzle of olive oil

1 garlic clove

splash balsamic vinegar

pinch caster sugar

pinch chopped thyme

salt and ground black pepper

CHICKPEA & APRICOT PATE:

250g dried chickpeas

150g dried apricots,

1 clove garlic, crushed

2 tbsp light tahini

1 tsp lemon juice

1 tsp tamari sauce

salt and ground black pepper

$1/2$ tsp paprika

$1/2$ tsp turmeric

SWEET RED PEPPER:

2 sweet red peppers, seeded and skinned

drizzle olive oil

sprinkle of paprika

salt and ground black pepper

fresh basil leaves

METHOD

Pre-heat oven to gas 6/200C/400F. Toss aubergine slices in large bowl with all other ingredients until fully coated. Lay evenly on a greased baking tray. Bake for 15-20 minutes until tender. **For pate,** soak 250g dried chickpeas overnight in water, drain and boil in fresh water for five minutes, then simmer for 50-60 minutes. Chop and add apricot for last 20 minutes of simmering. Drain chickpeas and apricot, reserving some of liquid. Place in food processor and add all other ingredients. Whizz until all ingredients are combined, adding some of cooking liquid if mixture too dry. **For peppers,** place the peppers under a hot grill turning over as each side is blackened. Allow to cool, and then scrape off the skin with a knife, then slice. **For relish,** sweat onion and garlic in olive oil for three minutes, add tomatoes, simmer for five minutes. Add other ingredients and cook for further two minutes. **To assemble,** you will need 12 teaspoons creme fraiche and 12 teaspoons breadcrumbs. On an oven tray, place 12 aubergine slices. Place a heaped tablespoon of chickpea and apricot pate on each slice. Top with remaining 12 slices of aubergine. Put a teaspoon of creme fraiche on each, followed by a sprinkling of breadcrumbs. Bake in pre-heated oven for 10-15 minutes. Place a clump of warm red pepper in the middle of each plate, topped with basil leaves, with three aubergine stacks around. Spoon on tomato relish.

QUINCE & MEDLAR

13 Castlegate, Cockermouth, Cumbria, CA13 9EU
Tel: 01900 823579, www.quinceandmedlar.co.uk

QUINCE & MEDLAR

Lemon and almond pudding

Serves 4

PUDDING:

1 large unwaxed lemon

150g sugar

3 eggs

125g ground almonds

1 level tsp baking powder

SYRUP:

225g caster sugar

juice and grated zest of one lemon

125ml water

4 cardamom pods

TO FINISH:

50g flaked almonds, lightly toasted

Method, pre-heat oven to gas 4/180C/350F. Put the lemon into a lidded pan, cover with water, bring to the boil and simmer for two hours. Allow to cool, then remove the pips and place the lemon, including the skin into a food processor, blend until a pulp. Grease and line four large ramekins with baking parchment. Beat the eggs and sugar together until pale and thick. Carefully add the ground almonds and baking powder. Add the lemon pulp and stir until blended. Pour mixture into prepared ramekins, place in a deep baking tray, half filled with water and bake for 50-60 minutes.

While puddings are baking, prepare the syrup. Place all syrup ingredients into a small pan and bring to the boil. Simmer for ten minutes. Then remove the cardamom pods.

When the puddings are baked, skewer the top, then pour over the syrup. Tip out onto the serving plate, sprinkle with flaked almonds and serve with cream, ice-cream or creme fraiche.

QUINCE & MEDLAR

13 Castlegate, Cockermouth, Cumbria, CA13 9EU
Tel: 01900 823579, www.quinceandmedlar.co.uk

ROTHAY MANOR

ROTHAY MANOR

Rothay Manor Hotel & Restaurant is situated in the heart of the Lake District, just a short walk from the centre of Ambleside. Set in its own landscaped gardens, the house was originally built in 1823 as a summer residence for a Liverpool shipping merchant and has been owned and personally managed by the Nixon family since 1967.

From its origins as a 'tiny hotel with a first class restaurant,' the hotel has grown a little, but the restaurant still retains the excellent reputation for first class cuisine, wine and service combined with a comfortable, relaxed and friendly atmosphere.

Head chef, Jane Binns, has been at the hotel for over 30 years and, together with her team, offers delicious seasonal menus with all dishes freshly prepared using local produce from the surrounding lakes and fells wherever possible, as well as from the nearby west coast.

The restaurant is light and airy with views over the garden, and well-spaced tables laid in a classical style with fine china, silver and crystal allow for 'intimate' dining. Catering for a maximum of 40 diners, there is also a private function room that can accommodate up to 34 diners.

With a long-standing reputation for the excellent buffet-style afternoon tea, the hotel has been mentioned in the Guardian newspaper as one of the '50 Best Places for Afternoon Tea'.

Listed in the 'Good Food Guide' for 38 years, Rothay Manor was recently the only hotel restaurant to be short-listed for the Cumbria Tourism 2008 'Taste' Awards.

Nigel Nixon

ROTHAY MANOR

Grilled salmon on a potato pancake

Serves 4

INGREDIENTS

4 salmon fillets

500g sautéed spinach

1 tbsp oil

125g crème fraiche

4 spring onions, chopped

slices of lemon and asparagus

(to garnish)

POTATO PANCAKE:

12g potato

2 eggs (beaten)

2 tsp plain flour

2 tsp cream

1 tsp milk

2 tsp oil

salt and pepper

1 teaspoon chopped herbs

METHOD

To prepare, boil potatoes until soft and mash. Add milk, cream, beaten egg, flour, chopped herbs and seasoning and mix well. Heat the oil in a pan. Put heat-proof rings filled with potato mixture in the pan and cook on both sides until golden brown.

Saute the spinach. Mix together the crème fraiche and the chopped spring onions. Grill the salmon. Top with sautéed spinach and crème fraiche mixture. Garnish with lemon and asparagus.

ROTHAY MANOR

Ambleside, Cumbria, LA22 OEH
Tel: 015394 33605, www.rothaymanor.co.uk

ROTHAY MANOR

Duo of pork roulade

Serves 6

INGREDIENTS

2 pork tender loins

12oz belly pork

12oz pork shoulder

1 onion

1 carrot

1 leek

2 tsp finely chopped fresh sage

3 pints chicken stock

salt and pepper

STUFFING:

2 onions, chopped

100g butter

2 tsp sage

400g breadcrumbs

2 eggs, beaten

salt and pepper

METHOD

To prepare, slowly roast the pork shoulder and belly pork with the above ingredients for approximately three hours at 180C. When cooked cool, separate meat from the fat and discard the fat. Shred the remaining meat and keep the stock. Sauté onions in the butter until soft then add the breadcrumbs and sage. Mix together with eggs, salt and pepper. Lay shredded meat on a layer of clingfilm. Place stuffing in a line in the middle of the meat and roll tightly. Place in fridge to chill. Meanwhile, reduce stock until it thickens slightly and then season to taste. Cut the pork fillet into medallions, approximately one inch thick. When ready to serve, slice the pork and stuffing roll and place in oven to reheat. Sauté pork fillet in a pan with a little oil and seasoning. Heat up the stock.

To assemble, place pork fillet on the plate, then place the rolled pork on top. Garnish with the sauce and vegetables of your choice. (Suggested vegetables: sweet potato mash piped on top of the pork, glazed carrots and asparagus).

ROTHAY MANOR

Ambleside, Cumbria, LA22 OEH
Tel: 015394 33605, www.rothaymanor.co.uk

ROTHAY MANOR

Pink Champagne and strawberry parfait

Serves 6

INGREDIENTS

SPONGE BASE:

1 egg, beaten

30g caster sugar

30g self-raising flour

PARFAIT:

4 egg yolks, beaten

150g caster sugar

300ml whipping cream

150ml pink Champagne

1 tsp caster sugar

6 medium-sized strawberries

6 x 60mm rings/moulds

METHOD

For sponge base, cream sugar and beaten egg until white. Fold in egg and flour a little at a time. Place in greased, small shallow tin and bake at 180C for five minutes. When cooked, cut into circles, place in bottom of ring/mould.

For the parfait, sprinkle teaspoon of caster sugar over the six strawberries and chop. Whisk the egg yolks until they double in size and are light in colour. Put sugar in a small pan with 100ml of water and boil until it 'threads' (ie stretches in strands – usually at 109C). Pour onto egg yolks a little at a time and keep whisking until cool. Egg yolks should have doubled in size again. Whisk cream until almost, but not quite, piping consistency. Fold into yolk and sugar mixture. Add pink Champagne and chopped strawberries. Place equal quantities of the mixture into the rings/moulds, on top of the cooked sponge base. Place in the freezer overnight.

ROTHAY MANOR

Ambleside, Cumbria, LA22 OEH
Tel: 015394 33605, www.rothaymanor.co.uk

THE SAMLING

THE SAMLING

What we strive for here at The Samling is to offer our guests not just lunch or dinner, but a true fine dining experience; a combination of food made from the highest quality local ingredients and prepared under the ever-watchful eye of head chef Nigel Mendham, a comprehensive wine list to suit every palate, personal service that is so effortless you hardly even notice it and surroundings that allow you to forget the real world, well, for a while at least…

Guests dine in one of our two small restaurants, both with views of Windermere lake, while drinks before and after the meal are served in the drawing room, where you can sink back into the sofas and lounge in front of a roaring log fire. The emphasis with dining, along with every other aspect of The Samling, is on informality and relaxation and is one of the reasons that guests keep returning time and again.

Lunch is available from noon until 1.30pm daily and dinner is available from 7pm until 9.30pm, although advance booking is required. Dietary requirements are no issue so long as we know prior to arrival and a vegetarian menu is always available. But don't just take our word for it, come and sample a true Samling experience for yourself.

Nigel Mendham of The Samling

THE SAMLING

Roast quail, terrine forestiere

Serves 6

INGREDIENTS

4 whole quail

4 quail eggs

TERRINE FORESTIERE:

1 ham shank

1 carrot, 1 leek, 2 celery stalks,

2 onions

150g chestnut mushrooms

150g button onions

50g flat parsley

50ml red wine

sprig thyme

clove garlic

MUSHROOM PUREE:

250g chestnut mushrooms

75g butter, unsalted

75ml double cream

salt and pepper

METHOD

To prepare, soak ham shank in water overnight. Remove shank from water and wash well, place in a pan of cold water and bring to the boil, refresh under cold water, place back into the pan with the vegetables listed above. Bring to the boil, skim off excess foam, and simmer for four hours, allow to cool in liquid. Pass off the liquid and reduce by half. While stock is reducing peel button onions, place in a pan with red wine, garlic and thyme, simmer until onions are soft, set aside. Bring a small pan of water to the boil, pick the parsley, wash and blanch in the boiling water for ten seconds, then put the parsley straight into iced water, strain and squeeze out excess water, set aside. Wash the mushrooms and dry in a cloth, heat oil in a sauté pan, add mushrooms and cook for two to three minutes, add a knob of butter, salt and continue cooking for another minute, allow mushrooms to cool on paper towel.

To build the terrine, pick down the ham hock, removing excess fat and sinew, place into a large mixing bowl with the mushrooms, onions and flat parsley, add the reduced stock and season to taste. Place in a suitable mould and press, place in the fridge preferably overnight.

For the quail, remove the winglets and legs, heat some oil in a pan, colour the quail for one minute on each side then add a knob of butter and roast for four to five minutes, take out and allow to rest. Remove the breasts from the carcass and season. Set aside.

For the mushroom puree, slice the chestnut mushrooms, foam the butter in a pan, add the mushrooms, a pinch of salt, cover and cook on a low heat for five minutes. Remove lid, add double cream, bring to the boil, check seasoning and blend until smooth. Pass through a sieve and set aside. Heat oil in a frying pan, break eggs into oil and gently fry until white is cooked. Remove from oil and set aside. **To serve,** assemble dish as photograph illustrates.

THE SAMLING

Ambleside Road, Windermere, Cumbria, LA23 1LR
Tel: 015394 31922, www.thesamlinghotel.co.uk

THE SAMLING

Loin of Herdwick mutton, langoustines, artichoke and confit potato

Serves 6

INGREDIENTS

Two racks of mutton (loins removed and trimmed)

1kg live langoustines

$^1/_2$ shoulder mutton, flat boned

$^1/_2$ pint water

$^1/_2$ pint white wine

sprig of thyme

6 white peppercorns

ARTICHOKE PUREE:

500g Jerusalem artichokes

75g butter

75ml double cream

lemon juice

GARNISH:

2 large potatoes

400g goose fat

sprig of thyme

250g spinach

mutton sauce

METHOD

Method, take the shoulder of mutton and place in a deep roasting tray, add white wine and water cover with parchment and tin foil, cook for four to five hours at 130C. **For the puree,** peel the artichokes and finely slice, foam the butter in a heavy-bottomed pan, add the artichokes, cover with a lid, and cook on a low heat until soft. When soft, add double cream, bring back to the boil, season and blend, pass through a fine sieve and set aside. Peel the potatoes and make each side flat, cut out the shape you require. Warm the goose fat and put the potatoes in and slow cook for 30 minutes, not allowing the oil to boil. To test if they are cooked use a cocktail stick. Pick the spinach, wash, set aside ready for cooking. When the mutton is cool enough to handle, pick the meat removing any excess fat and sinew, season, place between two layers of clingfilm and roll out to the correct thickness. Allow to set in the fridge. Peel the langoustines and put three on a cocktail stick. Place in the fridge until needed. For the loin of mutton, heat oil in a pan, seal off the mutton on all sides, add a knob of butter and continue cooking for four minutes, remove from pan and allow to rest for five minutes. To cook the langoustines, heat oil in a pan, add langoustines and cook on each side for 30 seconds, add a knob of butter and cook for a further 20 seconds, add a squeeze of lemon juice and remove from the pan. Next, cook the spinach, foam some butter in a large pan, add spinach and cook until it has wilted, remove from the pan and squeeze out excess liquid. **To serve,** plate the dish as the photo illustrates.

THE SAMLING

Ambleside Road, Windermere, Cumbria, LA23 1LR
Tel: 015394 31922, www.thesamlinghotel.co.uk

THE SAMLING

Serves 6

INGREDIENTS

APPLE PARFAIT:

8 egg yolks

200g sugar

400g apple puree

200ml double cream

100ml full fat milk

APPLE SORBET:

500g blush red apples

200g water

50g glucose

150g sugar

20ml lemon juice

APPLE PIE:

sweet pastry

apple compote, ready-bought

1 egg yolk

APPLE CRÈME BRULEE:

apple compote, ready-bought

175g double cream

2 egg yolks

12.5g sugar

vanilla pod

METHOD

For the apple parfait, whisk egg yolks and sugar together until tripled in volume, mix together double cream and milk and whisk until thick. Set aside. Add the apple puree to the egg mixture and fold in the cream and milk. Set in suitable containers and freeze.

For the apple sorbet, halve, quarter and core the apples and freeze. Boil together water glucose and sugar for two minutes, set aside. When apples are frozen, place in a blender, add syrup and blend until comes together. Add lemon juice to taste. Pass through a sieve and freeze.

For the apple pie, make one recipe of sweet pastry, roll out and line individual tart cases, blind bake, fill with apple compote, place a lid on top, egg wash and cook for 12-15 minutes at 170C.

For the crème brulee, bring to boil the double cream with the vanilla pod, set aside. Whisk egg yolks with sugar until thick and creamy, pour the cream over, whisking continuously, return to pan and cook until coats back of a spoon. Put apple compote into the bottom of the ramekins, pour over brulee mix and chill. Assemble the dish as pictured.

THE SAMLING

Ambleside Road, Windermere, Cumbria, LA23 1LR
Tel: 015394 31922, www.thesamlinghotel.co.uk

THE SUN INN

THE SUN INN

Mark and I visited Kirkby Lonsdale to order cheese for our wedding and saw The Sun Inn was for sale. We had a look round and fell in love with the old beams, oak floors and real fires of the run-down pub and quickly put in an offer to buy it. Initially we were turned down but we persisted and twelve months later in March 2006 we were finally handed the keys. The Sun needed a new roof, complete re-fitting of eleven bedrooms and bathrooms plus a complete overhaul of the bar and restaurant.

Now there is a stunning blend of contemporary and traditional at the 17th Century Sun Inn, by St Mary's church, in the centre of Kirkby Lonsdale. Flag and oak floors, real fires and cask ales combine with leather seating, rich colours and great wine in crystal glassware to create a relaxed modern inn.

Kirkby Lonsdale is an unspoilt market town in the heart of the Lune Valley; surrounded by wonderful farmland, it will be no surprise that we choose high quality local suppliers to provide us with the freshest ingredients for our menu. There is a great local butcher just two doors away and next door is an award-winning cheese shop and delicatessen. Fresh seasonal vegetables are picked and delivered within 24 hours; fish and seafood arrives daily. Head chef Sam Carter and his team prepare these ingredients with care, understanding and skill to create uncomplicated dishes in a modern style.

Lucy and Mark Fuller

THE SUN INN

Chicken livers and button mushrooms on toasted brioche

Serves 1

INGREDIENTS

1 slice brioche	25g butter
75g chicken livers	splash of oil for cooking
4-6 button mushrooms	100ml cream
pinch shallots, finely diced	35ml brandy
pinch garlic, finely chopped	knife point Dijon mustard
pinch parsley, chopped	drizzle truffle oil

METHOD

Method, pan button mushrooms, shallots and garlic in oil and butter. When mushrooms start to brown, add chicken livers, brandy and mustard.

Continue to cook for a couple of minutes then add cream and chopped parsley and reduce until sauce starts to thicken.

Toast brioche on both sides, drizzle one side with truffle oil and spoon chicken livers and mushrooms on top.

THE SUN INN

6 Market Square, Kirkby Lonsdale, Cumbria, LA26 2AU
Tel: 015242 71965, www.sun-inn.info

THE SUN INN

Breast of duck with rhubarb crumble

Serves 1

INGREDIENTS

1 duck breast	parsnip
⅓ stick rhubarb	onion
flour	celeriac
butter	swede
oats	sweet potato
demerara sugar	cream
potato	Cheddar cheese

METHOD

Method, poach rhubarb in stock syrup for two to three minutes until just soft. Rub flour, oats and butter together, add sugar to make crumble. Pan-fry duck breast skin-side down until golden then put into oven for eight to ten minutes. Allow to rest, then slice.

For root vegetable gratin, put cream, shallots, salt and pepper and potato into pan and cook for ten minutes. Remove the potato from the liquor and keep the cream stock. Place the potato in a deep tray, in layers with grated cheese and cream fix. Finish top layer with cheese. Press down firmly. Bake in oven for 45 minutes until browning a little on top. Put in fridge to cool overnight.

To serve, cut into squares and heat in oven.

THE SUN INN

6 Market Square, Kirkby Lonsdale, Cumbria, LA26 2AU
Tel: 015242 71965, www.sun-inn.info

THE SUN INN

Strawberries and cream

Serves 8/10

INGREDIENTS

CHAMPAGNE JELLY:

¹/₂ litre/500ml Champagne or sparkling wine

5 sheets gelatine

1 punnet strawberries

CREAM:

double cream

vanilla seeds

icing sugar

STRAWBERRY MOUSSE:

1 punnet strawberries

25ml grenadine

6 egg yolks

6oz icing sugar

100ml double cream

3 sheets gelatine

METHOD

For the Champagne jelly, slice or dice the strawberries. The shape and size will change the shape and texture of the dish. Soak the gelatine in the champagne and heat gently until liquid. Pour into the mould and layer in the strawberries. Allow to cool.

For the strawberry mousse, whisk the egg yolks and icing sugar over boiling water until thick and tight. Lightly whisk in the cream to the above. Blend and strain the strawberries. Fold the strawberries and cream together. Soak gelatine in cold water until soft and then gently heat until liquid. Fold into the strawberries and cream mix. Add to your mould and allow to cool.

For the cream, whisk together the double cream, vanilla seeds and icing sugar until sweet and thick. Quenelle with two spoons and place on top.

THE SUN INN

6 Market Square, Kirkby Lonsdale, Cumbria, LA26 2AU
Tel: 015242 71965, www.sun-inn.info

TEZA INDIAN CANTEEN & BAR

TEZA INDIAN CANTEEN & BAR

TEZA is Cumbria's leading Indian restaurant and boasts the very best of traditional and contemporary Indian cuisine, offering a dynamic and vibrant dining experience.

Numerous unprecedented steps were taken to set TEZA aside from everyone else. Along with a very sophisticated, stylish interior, the restaurant hosts an impressive cocktail bar and the theatrical show kitchen catches everyone's attention.

TEZA aims to push the boundaries of Indian cuisine to new heights. Taking the unparalleled step of bringing all the chefs with a background from the best five-star hotels from India puts TEZA head and shoulders above every other Indian operator in this region. The chefs have a deep understanding of Indian cuisine unlike any other.

Customers can listen to the sounds of Bollywood whilst tucking into authentic Indian cooking, with individual dishes inspired by the country's regional specialties. Using the best ingredients, the finest herbs and the most delicate spices, chefs prepare clean, simple and yet creative dishes with spectacular attention to detail. From much-loved classics to fragrant tandoori dishes, healthy options and contemporary creations, there's something for everyone.

Dedicated chefs explore the history and traditions of Indian cuisine, taking inspiration from all corners of the continent to deliver exciting fusions and exotic flavours.

For the curry connoisseur or those new to the cuisine, TEZA banishes any misconceptions of Indian cooking to bring a dining experience to Cumbria that is vibrant, exciting and unforgettable.

Jalf Ali

TEZA INDIAN CANTEEN & BAR

Citrus prawns

Serves 4

INGREDIENTS

FIRST MARINADE:

200g tiger king prawns

50ml oil

3g salt

15g ginger pod

15g garlic pod

lemon juice ($^1/_2$ lemon)

SECOND MARINADE:

4 kaffir lime leaf, chopped

3 sticks lemon grass, chopped

lemon juice ($^1/_2$ lemon)

15g brown sugar

8g paprika powder

4g red chilli powder

salt to taste

50ml oil

2g toasted cumin powder

3g garam masala powder

METHOD

Method, wash the prawns, soak and split in the middle using a knife. Then put the prawns in a bowl and coat with the first marinade and leave to rest. Moving on to the second marinade. Put all the ingredients into a separate bowl and mix together creating a paste and rest it for ten minutes. Add the prawns, (already coated with the first marinade) to the above paste and gently mix the paste ensuring a thorough marinade. Leave to rest for five minutes. Grill for seven to ten minutes until a golden brown colour. Serve with a salad.

TEZA INDIAN CANTEEN & BAR

4 Englishgate Plaza, Carlisle, Cumbria, CA1 1RP
Tel: 01228 525111, www.teza.co.uk

TEZA INDIAN CANTEEN & BAR

Meen Moilee – mustard seed and curry leaf spiced salmon in coconut milk

Serves 4

INGREDIENTS

FILLET:

200g salmon fillet

lemon juice ($^1/_2$ lemon)

salt (optional)

SPICES:

2g mustard seeds

2g coriander seeds

$^1/_2$ tsp turmeric

3-4 curry leaves

SAUCE:

50ml oil

2g mustard seeds

4-6 curry leaves

1 sliced red onion

25g ginger juliennes

4-6 sliced green chillies

$^1/_2$ tsp turmeric powder

600ml coconut milk

6 cherry tomatoes

lemon juice ($^1/_2$ lemon)

salt to taste

METHOD

Method, marinade the fillet with lemon juice and salt and leave it to rest for two to three minutes. In the meantime dry roast all the spices, let it cool and then powder them fine. Coat on one side of the fillet with the above spice mix and leave to rest for a few minutes.

For the sauce, heat oil and add the mustard seeds, as they crackle add the curry leaf and sauté for a minute. Add the sliced onion and ginger until they are translucent and then add the chillies. Add the turmeric and coconut milk, bring to the boil and then simmer for a further three to four minutes. Add cherry tomatoes, check for seasoning, add lemon juice and salt if required.

For the fillet, put a little oil in a hot pan and grill the already marinated fish, taking care not to burn the spices. Add the grilled salmon to the sauce and simmer for one to two minutes. Serve with steamed rice/steamed potatoes.

TEZA INDIAN CANTEEN & BAR

4 Englishgate Plaza, Carlisle, Cumbria, CA1 1RP
Tel: 01228 525111, www.teza.co.uk

TEZA INDIAN CANTEEN & BAR

Pista kulfi (pistachio flavoured Indian ice-cream)

Serves 4

INGREDIENTS

1 litre full cream milk	20g pistachio nuts (for garnish)
50ml sweet condensed milk	sugar (if required)
40g pistachio nuts	1g saffron

METHOD

Method, toast the 20g of pistachio nuts and then break into small pieces and leave to rest. Take 100ml of milk and the 40g of pistachio nuts and put both in to a blender to make a smooth paste. Mix the rest of the milk (900ml) and the condensed milk in a pan and boil until it has reduced to a quarter of the original amount. Remove from the hob and let it cool for a few minutes. By now it should have a feel of a heavy custard mix. Add saffron and the paste already made to the above along with sugar (if required). Cool the mixture by stirring frequently. Put the pistachio garnish into the bottom of the ice tray mould, and pour the above mixture and put into the freezer. In a few hours when it is hardened take it out of the mould, add some more pistachios, garnish and serve.

WINDER HALL
COUNTRY HOUSE

WINDER HALL
COUNTRY HOUSE

Tucked away in the village of Lorton, Winder Hall is one of Cumbria's oldest and most historically important buildings. Not surprisingly, the Winders who set up home here in the 14th Century, chose beautiful, sheltered parkland at the northern end of the Buttermere valley to be at the centre of their royal estate. The house has changed and grown over the years but parts of the building still date back to Tudor times.

The dining room was formed out of the Jacobean hall, embellished and made more intimate with oak panelling dating from the Arts and Crafts era. You would be forgiven for thinking this could lead to a formal and stuffy atmosphere but you would be wrong.

Ann and Nick Lawler who have owned Winder Hall since 2002 are not at all stuffy and their hospitality is genuinely relaxed and devoid of airs and graces. They somehow manage to juggle busy working lives with bringing up three children and a menagerie of animals (some of whom end up on the plate).

The prevailing attitude amongst their small team is looking after people is the most important thing, being proud of the local produce and cooking really nice food is important as well, but dinner without fun is like alcohol-free wine; completely pointless.

Nick Lawler

WINDER HALL
COUNTRY HOUSE

Spicy Solway shrimps

Serves 1

INGREDIENTS

brown shrimps

salted butter (or use the butter topping on potted shrimps)

paprika

fresh grated nutmeg

ground white pepper

cayenne pepper

METHOD

This is my take on a Cumbrian classic: potted shrimps. We use brown shrimps harvested by Ray the fisherman up on the Solway Firth. Of course Morecambe Bay shrimps are more famous but Ray's shrimps are even better! If you can't find brown shrimps, prawns will do but cook them longer so they shrivel up a bit and take on that firm tangy flavour that make our local shrimps so famous. We serve this as a warm starter with a little bit of salad and some melba toasts. Cooking is delightfully easy.

Melt a little bit of salted butter in a frying pan, add a generous handful of shrimps for each of your guests, then add paprika, ground white pepper, fresh grated nutmeg and a touch of cayenne pepper to taste. Make sure there is sufficient butter in the pan for the seasoning to evenly coat all the shrimps. Warm the shrimps through and the job's done.

WINDER HALL COUNTRY HOUSE

Low Lorton, Cockermouth, Cumbria, CA13 9UP
Tel: 01900 85107, www.winderhall.co.uk

WINDER HALL COUNTRY HOUSE

Slow-roast belly pork, pan-fried pork tenderloin, mashed root vegetables and caramelized apples

Serves 4-6

INGREDIENTS

2.5kg belly pork

large pork tenderloin

FOR THE GRAVY:

onion, celery, leeks and carrots

FOR THE MASHED ROOT VEGETABLES:

whatever is seasonal

dessert apples

demerara sugar

METHOD

This is a simple dish… but it does take time. You are aiming to gently melt the fat out of the joint leaving you with really sweet tender meat topped with the best crackling you will ever eat. Unfortunately, practice makes perfect with this dish. Give it a go, and then give it another go. We keep our own free-range Saddleback pigs at Winder Hall and I strongly recommend purchasing free-range or organic meat. The flavour is in the fat and you only get that with traditionally-reared pork. Score the skin on the belly. A Stanley knife is the best tool for the job. Place the belly on top of the chopped gravy vegetables in a baking tray. Add hot water, making sure the skin gets properly doused (it will give you better crackling in the end) but you are not casseroling this joint so leave the skin above the water level. Do not add salt – it will dry the meat out. Cover with tin foil and pop in low heat oven. Cook for five to seven hours or until most of the fat has dissolved out of the joint. You might want to baste the skin with the juices a couple of times during cooking. After cooking, strain the juices, discard the vegetables and then separate the fat from the gravy (there will be lots of fat). Reduce the gravy and maybe add a touch of redcurrant jelly for sweetness. Once you are happy that you have a really intense flavour, you can thicken with cornflour if you desire. To finish the belly off, pop the joint on a mesh, and place in a bain marie with the meat kept above the water level – you don't want to leach out any of the flavour now but this method will help keep the meat tender. Sprinkle the skin with salt and pepper and pop back in a hot oven for 30-45 minutes until you have fantastic crackling.

To make the caramelized apples, thinly slice the apples onto silicone paper. Generously sprinkle with demerara sugar and place under a grill. When the sugar has melted and begun to caramelize, turn the apples over and repeat the process.

In the restaurant we serve this with a couple of slices of pork tenderloin, pan-fried in butter, as illustrated.

WINDER HALL COUNTRY HOUSE

Low Lorton, Cockermouth, Cumbria, CA13 9UP
Tel: 01900 85107, www.winderhall.co.uk

WINDER HALL
COUNTRY HOUSE

Baked rhubarb on toasted brioche with blackcurrant Bellini and Cointreau and orange panna cotta

Serves 1

INGREDIENTS

stick rhubarb	icing sugar
caster sugar	cassis
brioche	sparkling wine

METHOD

A really easy pudding, but it's got all the right ingredients: not too filling, a little sweetness combined with the flavour and acidity of the fruit, texture and alcohol. First, cut the rhubarb into finger lengths and place on a baking tray. Generously sprinkle caster sugar on the rhubarb and add a dash of water to stop the rhubarb sticking. Cook in a medium oven for half an hour until the rhubarb is soft and slightly caramelized on top. Reserve the liquor. Cut your brioche into finger lengths, generously sprinkle with icing sugar and place under a grill. When the sugar has caramelized, turn the brioche over and repeat the process.

To serve, place the rhubarb on the brioche and add a little liquor to the plate. Add a shot glass to the plate with one third cassis (or strawberry syrup if you prefer) and two-thirds bubbly. Away you go!
In the restaurant we usually serve a baby panna cotta on the side, as illustrated.

WINDER HALL COUNTRY HOUSE

Low Lorton, Cockermouth, Cumbria, CA13 9UP
Tel: 01900 85107, www.winderhall.co.uk

ZEST

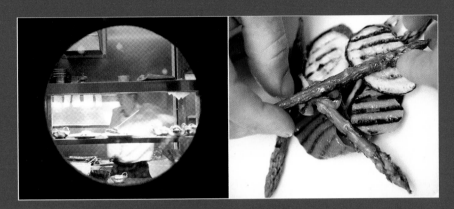

ZEST

Our aim is to provide good, tasty, affordable local food to a high standard. Both of our restaurants are situated in the Georgian harbour town of Whitehaven which has a rich maritime history and is gaining a reputation as an up-and-coming tourist destination. The recipes in this book are taken from our first Zest Restaurant where our menus are seasonally driven with the emphasis on carefully selected local produce, simply executed. We like the food to speak for itself. With our second restaurant, Zest Harbourside, we wanted to provide the relaxed, casual atmosphere of a bar café. We still, however, serve food to the highest quality which we like to describe as Northern-portion-sized tapas. The idea is to share a meal with friends or family with dishes such as wok chicken, a combination of sweet chilli chicken with crème fraiche and coriander, loads of garlic Cumbrian lamb and cobble tasty cheese tart – amongst others – to tempt your taste buds.

We pride ourselves on our friendly, professional and caring service that is provided by our staff who are predominantly Whitehaven-born and bred. We are extremely fortunate and proud to be well supported by local customers in the area. Why not come along and experience some Whitehaven charm for yourselves?

Emma and Ricky Andalcio, owners

ZEST

Seabass fillet with char-grilled vegetables and pesto

Serves 4

olive oil

$^1/_2$ aubergine, sliced

bunch of asparagus, trimmed

1 courgette, sliced

1 roasted red pepper, peeled and sliced

$^1/_4$ butternut squash, seeds removed and sliced

four skin-on and pin-boned fillets seabass (approximately 100g/4oz)

butter

salt and pepper

PESTO:

1 large bunch basil (you can use the stalks too, but cut off the very ends)

2 cloves garlic, peeled

75g fresh Parmesan cheese, roughly chopped

50g pine nuts, lightly toasted in a dry frying pan

pinch salt

100ml extra virgin olive oil

For the pesto, combine all ingredients and puree together. A hand blender or jug blender are good to use – or you could go old school and use a pestle and mortar. **For the vegetables,** drizzle the vegetables with oil, season them with salt and pepper, then char-grill in a smoking-hot griddle pan. The aubergine and butternut squash will take three to four minutes. The asparagus, pepper and courgette will take two to three minutes. **For the fish,** season the fish on both sides. Heat some olive oil and a little butter in a large frying pan. Put the fish in the pan skin-side down. Cook on a medium-high heat for four to six minutes, depending upon the thickness of the fish. Three-quarters of the time skin-side down then flip over for the remaining quarter of cooking time. Baste the fish from time to time with the oil and butter.

To serve, divide the vegetables between four serving plates, top with the seabass and drizzle over some pesto sauce.

ZEST

Zest Harbourside: 8 West Strand, Whitehaven, Cumbria, CA28 7LR Tel: 01946 66981
Zest Restaurant: Low Road, Whitehaven, Cumbria, CA28 9HS
Tel: 01946 692848 www.zestwhitehaven.com

ZEST

Venison steak with wild mushroom and leek Dauphinois potatoes

Serves 4

INGREDIENTS

4 x 225g/8oz venison haunch steaks

2 leeks, washed and finely shredded

200g fresh mixed wild mushrooms
(substitute dried if you can't get fresh,
but use less, about 45g)

600g new potatoes, sliced

300ml whipping or double cream

salt and pepper

olive oil

butter

METHOD

Method, pre-heat the oven to 180C. In a large saucepan, sauté the wild mushrooms in a little olive oil and butter for a few minutes then add a third of the leeks. Continue to sauté for a further few minutes and season with salt and pepper. Add the potatoes, stir around, then add the cream. Simmer for around three minutes and taste to check the seasoning. Divide the potato mixture between four, small individual-sized oven-proof dishes. Cook in the oven at 180C for approximately twenty minutes or until soft when a sharp knife is inserted into them. Lightly oil the venison steaks and season with salt and pepper. Heat a griddle pan until smoking hot and char-grill the venison for three to four minutes on each side to be served medium. Adjust the cooking time if necessary to your liking. Remove from the pan and set aside in a warm place to rest the meat. Heat a little oil and butter in a frying pan and add the rest of the leeks. Sauté until they are just cooked to retain their freshness and colour. Season them to taste.

To serve, place the potato pots on the plate. Make a bed of leeks then slice the venison and arrange on top of the leeks. Serve the dish with some red wine gravy if you wish.

ZEST

*Zest Harbourside: 8 West Strand, Whitehaven,
Cumbria, CA28 7LR Tel: 01946 66981
Zest Restaurant: Low Road, Whitehaven, Cumbria, CA28 9HS
Tel: 01946 692848 www.zestwhitehaven.com*

ZEST

Mixed berry cheesecake

Serves 10-12

INGREDIENTS

250g digestive biscuits, crushed

100g butter, melted

800g cream cheese

lemon zest and juice

100ml whipping or double cream

1 tsp vanilla extract

7 leaves gelatine

200g (approximately) sugar to taste

FOR THE SAUCE:

1 punnet each of strawberries, raspberries, blackcurrants and blackberries, all prepared/hulled.

300g (approximately) sugar to taste

dash cassis or blackcurrant cordial

dash water

METHOD

Line a 10-inch spring-form cake tin with clingfilm. In a bowl, combine the crushed biscuits with the melted butter. Spread this mixture over the base on the tin evenly, levelling out with the back of a metal spoon. Chill in the fridge.

For the sauce, keep back a few of each of the mixed berries for garnish for the cheesecake. Put the rest in a blender or food processor with a dash of water and cordial/cassis and two-thirds of the sugar (you can add more later depending on the sharpness of your fruit). Blend to a smooth puree. Taste to check the sweetness and adjust if necessary. Set aside.

For the cheesecake, in a small bowl, cover the gelatine leaves with cold water and leave to soak. In a large bowl, mix together the cream cheese, cream, vanilla and lemon zest and juice. Gradually beat in the sugar to your own taste. Once the gelatine is totally soft and malleable, drain it of water and squeeze out the excess. You will need 400ml of the sauce for the cheesecake mix (there should be some left over for garnish). Put around 75ml (from the 400ml) of the sauce in a small saucepan. Heat it up until bubbling, then remove from the heat and add the gelatine. Allow the gelatine to melt completely into the sauce. Add this gelatine mix and the rest of the 400ml sauce to the cheesecake mixture and fold in well to completely combine them together. Pour this mixture onto the biscuit base and return to the fridge to chill for at least four hours, preferably overnight.

To serve, cut the cheesecake into even-sized portions. Pour over some of the remaining sauce and garnish with a few reserved berries and a caramel wafer if you wish.

ZEST

Zest Harbourside: 8 West Strand, Whitehaven,
Cumbria, CA28 7LR Tel: 01946 66981
Zest Restaurant: Low Road, Whitehaven, Cumbria, CA28 9HS
Tel: 01946 692848 www.zestwhitehaven.com

LARDER

FOOD has become a major draw for visitors to the Lake District, Cumbria, with the food and drink sector now worth an estimated £180 million each year to the Cumbrian economy.

Visitors to any destination now expect the highest quality throughout all aspects of their experience; from their accommodation, the things to see and do, and the appearance of an area, right through to the standard of the food and drink on offer. The Lake District,

Cumbria is synonymous with top quality food and drink and our local produce and local food initiatives play a crucial role in ensuring that this sector continues to prosper. For hundreds of years, our living, breathing landscape has provided the perfect environment for growing and rearing a mouth-watering range of delicious local foods, which adds to the unique heritage and culture of the county.

It comes as no surprise then that The Lake

District, Cumbria boasts a phenomenal number of restaurants, pubs and cafés which pride themselves on their use of local produce; including three Michelin-starred restaurants – truly from 'field to fork.'

At whatever time of year you visit the Lakes, make sure you're hungry!

For further information on food and drink in the Lake District, Cumbria, visit www.golakes.co.uk

BEVERAGES

COWMIRE HALL
www.cowmire.co.uk
Cowmire Hall, Crosthwaite, Kendal, Cumbria, LA8 8JJ. Tel: 01539 568200
The damson orchards of the Lyth Valley and surrounding area are famous for their distinctive, purple fruit in the autumn. When skilfully married to London Gin at Cowmire Hall the damsons produce a delicious gin which, not being too sweet, can be served as an aperitif, and as a liqueur.

CUMBRIAN LEGENDARY ALES
www.cumbrianlegendaryales.com
Old Hall Brewery, Hawkshead, Ambleside, LA22 0QF. Tel: 01539 436436
Beers named after famous Cumbrian characters of the past. Brewed on the shores of Esthwaite Water.

HARDKNOTT BREWERY (WOOLPACK INN)
www.woolpack.co.uk
Boot, Eskdale, Cumbria, CA19 1TH.
Tel: 01946 723230
The Woolpack Inn is steeped in history, dating from 1578 or before. The Victorian facade hides much older walls of granite and rock from the Roman fort and the attic secretly guards ancient oak trusses.

KESWICK BREWING COMPANY
www.keswickbrewery.co.uk
The Old Brewery, Brewery Lane, Keswick, CA12 5BY. Tel: 01768 780700
Phil and Sue Harrison started up the 10-barrel brewery in the aptly-named Old Brewery. This is the site of the Old Allinsons Brewery which ceased in 1897. Their first brew was exhibited at the Cumbria Life Food and Drink Festival 2006. It was then on sale as Thirst Run at the Keswick Beer Festival and The Dog and Gun, Keswick, June 2006. They produce cask real ales and also have bottled beers for sale.

STRAWBERRY BANK LIQUEURS LTD
www.strawberrybankliqueurs.co.uk
Wood Yeat Barn, Crosthwaite, Kendal, LA8 8HX. Tel: 01539 568812

We produce damson beer and damson gin from the fruit grown in our own orchard and those of other growers in the Lyth Valley. We also produce other fruit liqueurs from pure fruit juices blended in the Lyth Valley.

ULVERSTON BREWING CO
www.ulverstonbrewing.co.uk
Diamond Buildings, Pennington Lane, Lindal-in-Furness, Ulverston, LA12 0LA.
Tel: 01229 584280
Ulverston Brewing Company was set up in early 2006 by Paul Swann and Anita Garnett. The brewery is situated on the outskirts of Ulverston in a building that once housed the winding gear for Lindal Moor Mining Company. Our brewery beers have mostly been named in tribute to one of Ulverston's famous sons, Stan Laurel, and denote some of the best-known moments from Laurel and Hardy films.

BAKERY

BRYSON'S OF KESWICK
www.brysonsofkeswick.co.uk
42 Main Street, Keswick, CA12 5JD
Tel: 01768 772257
Bryson's craft bakery is renowned for the quality of its fresh bakery products. Baking fresh goods every day, this company produces the widest range of breads, cakes, morning goods and cream cakes that you will see. Specialities include Lakeland plum bread and Borrowdale tea bread.

MOODY BAKER CO-OP LTD
3 West View, Front Street, Alston, Cumbria, CA9 3SF. Tel: 01434 382003
We are a bakery co-operative, producing many varied specialities. Our breads, cakes, snacks, biscuits etc are all produced using the most natural and local ingredients possible.

THE STAFF OF LIFE
www.artisanbreadmakers.co.uk
staffoflife@ukf.net
Staff of Life Bakery, 2 Berry's Yard, Kendal, LA9 4AB.
Tel: 01539 738606
Artisan baker. We make many different specials using wheat, rye, barley and oats either on their own or as multigrains.

VILLAGE BAKERY
www.village-bakery.com
Melmerby, Penrith, Cumbria. CA10 1HE.
Tel: 01768 881811
Natural good taste is the secret of our success. A pioneering organic bakery brand established nearly 30 years ago, we still maintain a unique reputation for quality and product innovation. We use natural processes, artisan methods, renewable energy and interesting ingredients to make our award-winning organic and special dietary ranges.

CONFECTIONERY
Chocolatehouse 1657
www.chocolatehouse1657.co.uk
54 Branthwaite Brow,
Kendal, LA9 4TX. Tel: 01539 740702
Our chocolate shop is perched above the cobbled streets of Branthwaite Brow, and here you will discover an Aladdin's cave of chocolates and gifts. Visit our chocolate restaurant and enjoy chocolate drinks, gateaux and ice creams.

KENNEDYS FINE CHOCOLATES
The Old School, Orton, Penrith, Cumbria, CA10 3RU. Tel: 01539 624781
Manufacturers and retailers of fine hand-made chocolates.

SAUNDERS CHOCOLATES
www.saunderschocolates.co.uk
Rheged Centre, Redhills, Penrith, Cumbria, CA11 0DQ. Tel: 01768 860098
We have been making fine chocolates in our kitchen workshop since the summer of 2003. Visitors to our shop within Rheged, near Penrith, can watch us making our unique chocolates and truffles.

TRUFFLES
www.truffleschocolates.co.uk
2 Kingswater Close, Brampton, CA8 1PD.
Tel: 01697 742539
We produce hand-made British gourmet chocolate truffles, taking only the very finest chocolates, real fruit and local fresh Cumbrian cream. Each gourmet chocolate is entirely hand-made and takes up to three days to produce.

DAIRY

CUMBERLAND DAIRY
www.thecumberlanddairy.co.uk
Knock Cross, Long Marton, Appleby,
CA16 6BX. Tel: 08453 707 020
Producer of Cumbrian cheeses – Blengdale
Blue, Roegill Red, Cobble Tasty, Keldthwaite
Gold. You can buy the cheeses for your own
table from specialist cheese shops and
delicatessens across Cumbria. We are also
found at local food fairs, agricultural shows
and farm shops.

HOLKER FARM CHEESE
www.holkerfoodhall.co.uk
Holker Estates Co Ltd, The Estates Office,
Cark-in-Cartmel, Cumbria, LA11 7PH.
Tel: 01539 559084
The latest addition to the Foods of Excellence
range comes from Martin Gott who moved to
the Holker Estate with his milking sheep
flock. Martin produces various ewes' milk
cheeses and has won awards for his
products and has a regular market for his
cheeses in London.

LOW SIZERGH BARN
www.lowsizerghbarn.co.uk
Low Sizergh Farm, Sizergh, Kendal, Cumbria,
LA8 8AE. Tel: 015395 60426
We have a farm shop, tea room, craft gallery
and farm trail on our organic dairy farm near
the Lake District National Park. The farm shop
is filled with one of the best selections of local
and speciality foods in Cumbria, with farm
products – our own organic Kendal cheese,
organic eggs and ice-cream made from our
milk – taking pride of place.

THE LAKE DISTRICT
CHEESE COMPANY
www.lakedistrictcheesecompany.co.uk
The Lake District Creamery, Aspatria, Wigton,
CA7 2AR. Tel: 01697 320218
The Lake District Cheese Company is a farmer
owned co-operative set in the heart of the
magnificent Cumbrian countryside, producing
a range of premium cheeses crafted with milk
from local dairy farms. Over the last 120 years,
generations of families have worked at our
creamery and it is these dedicated, highly
skilled cheese makers that capture the depth
of flavour that make our cheeses unique.

THORNBY MOOR DAIRY
Crofton Hall, Thursby, Carlisle, Cumbria,
CA5 6QB. Tel: 016973 45555
Established in 1979, Thornby Moor Dairy
produces a range of cows', goats' and ewes'
milk cheeses using raw milk sourced from
single herds within Cumbria. Carolyn
Fairburn has developed her range of
handmade cheeses relying on traditional
methods of production and maturation to
produce a natural, wholesome food.

FARM SHOPS

COUNTRY CUTS
ORGANIC MEATS
www.country-cuts.co.uk
Bridge End Farm, Santon Bridge, Holmrook,
CA19 1UY. Tel: 019467 26256
Family-run organic farm producing clover-fed,
mature Aberdeen Angus/Limousin beef,
tender hill and lowland mutton and lamb.
Delicious pork sausages, bacons and hams
from outdoor Saddleback pigs. Free- range
poultry, organic and duck eggs and trout.
Also non-organic fruit and vegetables. Farm
shop, mail order and local outlets.

GREYSTONE HOUSE FARM
SHOP & TEAROOM
www.greystonehousefarm.co.uk
Greystone House, Stainton, Penrith,
CA11 0EF. Tel: 01768 866952
Award-winning farm shop and tearoom and
producer of organic beef and lamb. One of
Rick Stein's food heroes

HOWBARROW ORGANIC FARM
www.howbarroworganic.co.uk
Howbarrow Farm, Cartmel, Grange over
Sands, Cumbria, LA11 7SS.
Tel: 015395 36330
Howbarrow Organic Farm produces food to
the rigorous standards set by the Soil
Association. We produce lamb, beef and
seasoned poultry as well as an extensive range
of in-season vegetable, salads and herbs. We
offer a home delivery service, box scheme and
self-select home shopping service for over 600
lines of organic food. We operate an open farm
policy and actively encourage visitors.

KITRIDDING FARM
www.kitridding.co.uk
Kitridding Farm, Lupton, Kirkby Lonsdale,
LA6 2QA. Tel: 015395 67484
Traditionally-reared Swaledale lamb,
traditionally-reared home-bred beef and
home-made sausages.

NATLAND MILLBECK FARM
& ICE-CREAM PARLOUR
www.millbeckicecream.co.uk
Natland Millbeck Farm, Natland Millbeck
Lane, Kendal, LA9 7LH.
Tel: 01539 729333
We are a working family dairy farm milking
120 Holstein Friesian dairy cows twice daily.
This milk is then used to make our delicious
ice-cream here at the parlour. In addition, the
Millbeck herd of pedigree Aberdeen Angus
cows provides quality meat for sale through
our farm shop.

PLUMGARTHS FOOD PARK
AND FARM SHOP
www.plumgarths.co.uk
Crook Road, Kendal, Cumbria,
LA8 8QJ. Tel: 01539 736136
Plumgarths is a business specialising in local
produce just within the Lake District National

Park. Developed by the Geldards, a traditional
Cumbrian farming family, Plumgarths provides
you with the opportunity to purchase a wide
range of natural, wholesome, high-quality food
sourced from local farmers and other small-
scale suppliers located throughout Cumbria.

RAYNE COTTAGE
Gaisgill, Penrith, CA10 3UD.
Tel: 01539 624129
We breed Gloucester spot pigs, Aberbeen
Angus beef and lamb on our farm near Tebay.
You can buy our home-made sausages and
bacon direct from the farm.

SILLFIELD FARM
Sillfield Farm, Endmoor, Kendal, Cumbria,
LA8 0HZ. Tel: 015395 67609
Farm-made food products from our own
outdoor free-range rare-breed pigs and wild
boar. Products include dry-cured bacon,
Cumberland and wild boar sausages,
Cumberland dry-cured hams, prosciutto and
salamis, black pudding, Westmorland cheeses
and a range of naturally smoked products.

WELLINGTON JERSEYS
ICE-CREAM & TEAROOMS
Wellington Farm, Cockermouth, Cumbria,
CA13 0QU. Tel: 01900 822777
The Stamper family make a wide range of ice-
cream using milk from our own herd of
pedigree Jersey cattle. We also sell freshly-
made traybakes, home-cooked meals and offer
a daily specials board which can all be sampled
in our fully licensed tearooms and farm shop.

FISH

BESSY BECK TROUT FISHERY
www.bessybecktrout.co.uk
Greenhead House, Newbiggin on Lune,
Kirkby Stephen, CA17 4LY.
Tel: 015396 23303
Trout farm and producer of fish terrines and
pates. Our farm shop is now fully open and
stocked with really fine local produce,
venison, herb-fed beef and lamb, cakes,
fudge, salad dressings and lots more.

FURNESS FISH POULTRY
& GAME SUPPLIES
www.morecambebayshrimps.com
Moor Lane, Flookburgh, Grange-over-Sands,
LA11 7LS. Tel: 015395 59544
Morecambe Bay potted shrimps in butter with
a flavour of their own, caught locally by
fishermen using tractors and dragging nets
along the sea floor. Boiled and cooked in
butter with our own spices. All types of local
game including a unique selection of game
pies/smoked fish/meals.

SOLWAY SHELL FISHERIES LTD
Windmill, Black Dyke,
Silloth on Solway, CA7 4PZ.
Oyster farm off the Solway coast.

MEAT

FAR EDGE ORGANIC
www.faredge-organic.com
Far Branthwaite Edge, Branthwaite,
Workington, CA14 4TB. Tel: 01900 602428
A family-run business selling organic beef
and lamb direct to the public and the catering
trade.

GREYSTONE HOUSE FARM SHOP & TEAROOM
www.greystonehousefarm.co.uk
Greystone House, Stainton, Penrith
CA11 0EF. Tel: 01768 866952
Award-winning farm shop and tea room and
producer of organic beef and lamb. One of
Rick Stein's food heroes

HADRIAN ORGANICS LTD
www.hadrianorganics.co.uk
Grainbrow, Hethersgill,
Carlisle, CA6 6HD. Tel: 01228 675252
Hadrian Organics is the first Cumbrian
co-operative of organic producers. We
formed to sell direct to the public a wide
range of quality, organic farm produce
naturally reared, grown and produced in
North Cumbria, within striking distance of
Hadrian's Wall, a beautiful, historic and fertile
landscape.

HERB FED BEEF & LAMB
Adamthwaite, Ravenstonedale, Kirkby
Stephen, Cumbria, CA17 4NW.
Tel: 01539 623207
Breeds beef and lamb on protected pastures
with rare herbs and flowers in the Howgills.
Attends farmers' markets and sells direct to
hotels and recently the YHA.

HOLKER SALT MARSH LAMB
Holker Estates Co Ltd, The Estates Office,
Cark-in-Cartmel, Cumbria, LA11 7PH.
Tel: 01539 558313
Lamb reared entirely on the Cumbrian
saltmarshes is available directly from the
Holker Estate. Saltmarsh lamb has long been
regarded as a rare delicacy in French
restaurants for its unique and striking flavour.
Whole and half lamb delivered to your door.

KENDAL ROUGH FELL SHEEP MEAT PRODUCERS
High Carlingill, Tebay, Penrith,
CA10 3XX
Tel: 01539 624661.
We sell half and quarter packs of lamb from
Kendal's local breed of sheep, kept
traditionally. Roaming free on the fells, they
graze the natural herbage to give meat with a
quality flavour. Producers abide by modern
welfare standards.

KITRIDDING FARM
www.kitridding.co.uk
Kitridding Farm, Lupton, Kirkby Lonsdale,
LA6 2QA. Tel: 01539 567484
Traditionally-reared Swaledale lamb,

traditionally-reared home-bred beef and
home-made sausages.

LOWTHER ORGANIC
www.lowtherparkfarms.co.uk
Lowther Park Farms, The Estate Office,
Lowther, Penrith, CA10 2HG
Tel: 01931 712407
Lowther Park is a 3,000-acre upland
grassland farm in the Lake District National
Park. The Lowther family has been producing
quality food on the estate for nearly 800
years. This tradition continues and has been
enhanced since 2001 with the conversion of
the farm to organic production methods.

HERBS & SPICES

THE CHILLI PEPPER COMPANY
www.hotseeds.co.uk
Stony Bridge, Cark-in-Cartmel, LA11 7PE.
Tel: 01539 558110
Suppliers of chilli seeds. All things chilli
including chilli chocolate, marinades, dips,
and sauces. They use a range of locally
sourced ingredients in their products.

COOKED MEAT & PIES

BURBUSH PENRITH LTD
www.burbushs.co.uk
The Eden Game Bakery, Gilwilly Road,
Gilwilly Ind Est, Penrith, CA11 9BL.
Tel: 01768 863841
Burbush's of Penrith Ltd are pie-makers with
a 20-year history to be envied. All our pies
are made, finished and packed by hand and
using locally sourced, quality and traceable
ingredients.

RICHARD WOODALL
www.richardwoodall.co.uk
Lane End, Waberthwaite,
Millom, LA19 5YJ.
Tel: 01229 717237
Nestling between the western edge of the
Lakeland fells and the Irish Sea lies the sleepy
backwater village of Waberthwaite. This is
home to Richard Woodall, one of the oldest
family businesses still in existence. The
company, currently run by seventh and eighth
generation family members, is renowned for
its much-acclaimed, traditionally cured hams,
bacon and sausages.

SILLFIELD FARM
www.sillfield.co.uk
Sillfield Farm, Endmoor, Kendal Cumbria, LA8
0HZ. Tel: 01539 567609
Farm-made food products from our own
outdoor free-range rare-breed pigs and wild
boar.

THE PIE MILL
www.piemill.co.uk
Unit 16, Blencathra Business Centre,
Threlkeld, Keswick, CA12 4TR.
Tel: 01768 779994
A superb range of quality hand-made pies

using only the best local ingredients. Tried
and tested at the Mill Inn for years.

PRESERVES, RELISHES, HONEY

BORDER COUNTY FOODS
Kingmoor Barn, Kingmoor Park,
Carlisle, CA6 4SP.
Tel: 01228 672020
Producer of award-winning Cumberland
sausages made from rare-breed pork and
one of Rick Stein's food heroes. Also cured
and speciality meats sold through local
farmers' markets. North West fine food
producer of the year, in 2004.

CONISTON COUNTRY KITCHEN LARDER
www.coniston-lodge.com
Coniston Lodge, Coniston, Cumbria,
LA21 8HH. Tel: 01539 441201
Award-winning hand-made produce.
Chutneys, jams, marmalade and Coniston
Lodge gingerbread. You can buy this
produce at Coniston Lodge, Coniston, or by
mail order. Beautiful hampers available.
Orders for luxury Christmas puddings can be
taken in advance.

COUNTRY FLAVOUR
www.country-flavour.co.uk
15 High Street, Kirkby Stephen,
Cumbria, CA17 4SG.
Tel: 01768 371124
Our family business, established in 1948
uses the expertise of three generations to
produce fudge, toffee, lemon cheese,
marmalade, herb jellies, jam from local fruit
and rum butter. All our products are
home-made by us in Kirkby Stephen. We
also sell at local markets, shows and
wholesale throughout Cumbria.

CUMBERLAND MUSTARD
www.cumberlandmustard.com
16 Hillhouse Lane, Alston,
Cumbria, CA9 3TN.
Tel: 01434 381135
We were established in 1984 in Alston
making high-quality, unique honey mustards
and a range of pickles and vinaigrettes using
our special raspberry vinegar. New lines
always appearing. We offer own label and
own recipe service with full traceability on all
products. Retail and catering sizes.

DEMELS
www.demels.co.uk
Cross Lane, Ulverston,
Cumbria, LA12 9DQ. Tel: 01229 580580
Producers of tantalising award-winning
chutneys and pickle, hand-made to
traditional Sri Lankan recipes. A range of ten
varieties available by mail order or in retail
outlets throughout the North West and
expanding South. Excellent with sandwiches,
as a marinade or dip and a treat with curries.

HAWKSHEAD RELISH CO LTD

www.hawksheadrelish.com
The Square, Hawkshead
Ambleside, LA22 0NZ.
Tel: 01539 436614
The Hawkshead Relish Company is a producer of over 100 award-winning hand-made relishes, pickles and preserves, mustards, sauces, flavoured oils and vinegars. Hand-made using the finest, freshest ingredients. All available in the shop in Hawkshead (which is open every day) or at selected stockists throughout Cumbria and through the online shop. Winners of Specialist Producer of the Year 2005.

LIZZIE'S HOME MADE

www.fruttacotta.co.uk
The Bank, Dockray,
Penrith, CA11 0LG.
Tel: 01768 482487
A delicious pudding of figs, apricots and prunes in a Cumbrian spiced rum syrup. The product range consists of Cumbrian frutta cotta mostarda, Cumbrian frutta cotta, dried apricots in a spiced amaretto syrup, posh prunes and Primi prunes.

NOOK FARM HONEY

www.nookfarmhoney.co.uk
Nook Farm, Bailey, Cumbria,
TD9 0TR. Tel: 01697 748317
The finest English speciality honeys. Wildflower honey, borage honey and balsam honey. Our clear runny Cumbrian wildflower honey is delicious. Nook Farm bees forage in the unspoilt countryside of Cumbria.

WILD AND FRUITFUL

Hillside, Cuddy Lonning, Wigton,
Cumbria, CA7 0AA.
Tel: 01697 344304
Wild and Fruitful produces small, unique batches of hand-made jams, jellies, chutneys, oils, vinegars and salts using local, hand-picked, unsprayed ingredients where possible, in unusual combinations as well as old favourites. Jars are labelled with the origin of ingredients (sometimes down to a specific tree!) and exciting alternative uses.

PUDDING ROOM

Old Brown Howe Barn, Water Yeat, Coniston, Cumbria, LA12 8DW.
Tel: 01229 885670
A special range of desserts using the finest ingredients. Our recipes include the best quality Belgian chocolate, to be enjoyed by connoisseurs of fine dining.

SARAH NELSON'S GRASMERE GINGERBREAD SHOP

www.grasmeregingerbread.co.uk
Church Cottage, Grasmere, Ambleside,
Cumbria, LA22 9SW. Tel: 01539 435428
For the last 150 years Sarah Nelson's Original Celebrated Grasmere Gingerbread has been baked fresh every day to a secret recipe.

Although world-famous it can only be purchased from the shop in Grasmere or through the mail order service. Awarded Gold Taste Award for Traditional Cumberland Rum Butter. Also stockist of other Made in Cumbria products.

SWEET HOME

Briardale, Millans Park, Ambleside,
Cumbria, LA22 9AG.
Tel: 01539 434070
Delicious hand-made puddings, boasting a big-time fan base of 'those in the know', now available commercially. Currently on offer are chocolate and cherry, chocolate and damson, cranberry and orange and date and sticky toffee puddings, with more favourites to follow.

ULTIMATE PLUM PUDDING CO LTD

www.ultimateplumpudding.co.uk
Units 9-10, Beezan Road Trading Estate,
Kendal, LA9 6BW.
Tel: 01539 734144
Infinitely flexible, our light and delicious luxury Christmas pudding is available in our attractive gold retail pack or it can easily be personalised for retail private label, fundraising, corporate gifts and promotions or just a special family gift. We have in-house facilities for printing and designing glossy labels for even the smallest order.

SMOKED FOODS

BORDER COUNTY FOODS

Kingmoor Barn, Kingmoor Park,
Carlisle, CA6 4SP. Tel: 01228 672020
Producer of award-winning Cumberland sausages made from rare breed pork and one of Rick Stein's food heroes. Also cured and speciality meats sold through local farmers' markets. North West fine food producer of the year in 2004.

LAKELAND BARN ARTISAN FOODS

Howestone Barn, Whinfell,
Kendal, Cumbria, LA8 9EQ.
Tel: 01539 824373
Producer of highly crafted, natural products: dry-cure bacon, traditional prime meat sausage and continental-style charcuterie. Production is on a small scale, based on principles of responsible husbandry. Traditional breeds, slowly reared outdoors in Cumbria. Additionally, a range of seasonal preserves.

OLD SMOKE HOUSE & TRUFFLES CHOCOLATES

www.the-old-smokehouse.co.uk
Brougham Hall, Brougham,
Penrith, Cumbria, CA10 2DE.
Tel: 01768 867772
At the Old Smokehouse we produce high-quality smoked food with a wonderful flavour. We take local produce, which we brine in our own recipes of herbs and spices. We then

individually smoke all our products by either cold smoking or smoke-roasting them over oak in the traditional manner. We have won 14 Great Taste Awards since 2002, including several gold awards for our duck breast, Penrith pepperpot sausage and Fellman sausage. We take care and great pride in producing our foods and we are confident that you and your friends will enjoy them.

RICHARD WOODALL LTD

www.richardwoodall.co.uk
Lane End, Waberthwaite, Millom, LA19 5YJ.
Tel: 01229 717237
Nestling between the western edge of the Lakeland fells and the Irish Sea lies the sleepy backwater village of Waberthwaite. This is home to Richard Woodall, one of the oldest family businesses still in existence. The company, currently run by seventh and eighth generation family members, is renowned for its much acclaimed, traditionally-cured hams, bacon and sausages.

SADDLEBACK FOODS AND SMOKERIE

www.saddlebackfoods.co.uk
Scarfoot, Plumpton, Penrith,
Cumbria, CA11 9PF.
Tel: 01768 885599
Saddleback Foods and Smokerie has now moved back to the family farm where we can offer fresh meat and poultry alongside our existing range of smoked produce, pates and ready meals.

With thanks to Cumbria Tourism, Windermere Road, Staveley, Kendal, LA8 9PL.
Tel: 01539 822222 www.golakes.co.uk

CONTRIBUTORS

BROADOAKS
Bridge Lane, Troutbeck, Windermere, Cumbria, LA23 1LA
Tel: 015394 45566
www.broadoakscountryhouse.co.uk

THE COTTAGE IN THE WOOD
Braithwaite, Nr Keswick, Cumbria, CA12 5TW
Tel: 017687 78409
www.thecottageinthewood.co.uk

DALE LODGE HOTEL
Grasmere, Cumbria, LA22 9SW
Tel: 015394 35300
www.dalelodgehotel.co.uk

THE GLASS HOUSE RESTAURANT
Rydal Road, Ambleside, Cumbria, LA22 9AN
Tel: 015394 32137
www.theglasshouserestaurant.co.uk

GOOD TASTE CAFÉ
19 Lake Road, Keswick, Cumbria, CA12 5BS
Tel: 017687 75973 www.simplygoodtaste.co.uk

JERICHOS AT WAVERLEY
College Road, Windermere, Cumbria, LA23 1BX
Tel: 015394 42522
www.jerichos.co.uk

LUCYCOOKS
Mill Yard, Staveley, Kendal, Cumbria, LA8 9LR
Tel: 015394 32288
www.lucycooks.co.uk

MORREL'S RESTAURANT
34 Lake Road, Keswick, Cumbria, CA12 5DQ
Tel: 017687 72666
www.morrels.co.uk

NO 10 RESTAURANT
Eden Mount, Carlisle, Cumbria, CA3 9LY
Tel: 01228 524183
www.no10limited.co.uk

THE PHEASANT
Bassenthwaite Lake, Nr Cockermouth,
Cumbria, CA13 9YE
Tel: 017687 76234
www.the-pheasant.co.uk

PUNCH BOWL INN
Crosthwaite, Lyth Valley, Cumbria, LA8 8HR
Tel: 015395 68237
www.the-punchbowl.co.uk

QUINCE & MEDLAR
13 Castlegate, Cockermouth, Cumbria, CA13 9EU
Tel: 01900 823579
www.quinceandmedlar.co.uk

ROTHAY MANOR
Ambleside, Cumbria, LA22 OEH
Tel: 015394 33605
www.rothaymanor.co.uk

THE SAMLING
Ambleside Road, Windermere, Cumbria, LA23 1LR
Tel: 015394 33605, www.thesamlinghotel.co.uk

THE SUN INN
6 Market Square, Kirkby Lonsdale, Cumbria, LA26 2AU
Tel: 015242 71965
www.sun-inn.info

TEZA INDIAN CANTEEN & BAR
4 Englishgate Plaza, Carlisle, Cumbria, CA1 1RP
Tel: 01228 525111
www.teza.co.uk

WINDER HALL COUNTRY HOUSE
Low Lorton, Cockermouth, Cumbria, CA13 9UP
Tel: 01900 85107
www.winderhall.co.uk

ZEST
8 West Strand, Whitehaven, Cumbria, CA28 7LR
Tel: 01946 66981,
Low Road, Whitehaven, Cumbria, CA28 9HS
Tel: 01946 692848
www.zestwhitehaven.com